The Twisted Path of The Hidden Saint: An Occult Tale of The Baal Shem Tov

By

BARAK A. BASSMAN

This book is a work of fiction. Names, characters, places and incidents are either the product of the author's imagination or are used fictitiously. Any resemblance to actual persons, living or dead, or to actual events or locales is entirely coincidental.

THE TWISTED PATH OF THE HIDDEN SAINT:
AN OCCULT TALE OF THE BAAL SHEM TOV
Copyright © 2023 BARAK A. BASSMAN. All rights reserved, including the right to reproduce this book, or portions thereof, in any form. No part of this text may be reproduced, transmitted, downloaded, decompiled, reverse engineered, or stored in or introduced into any information storage and retrieval system, in any form or by any means, whether electronic or mechanical without the express written permission of the author. The scanning, uploading, and distribution of this book via the Internet or via any other means without the permission of the author and publisher is illegal and punishable by law. Please purchase only authorized electronic editions and do not participate in or encourage electronic piracy of copyrighted materials.

The publisher does not have any control over and does not assume any responsibility for author or third-party websites or their content.

Cover designed by Telemachus Press, LLC

Cover art: ©Copyright iStock_481079234_THEPALMER

Publishing services by Telemachus Press, LLC
7652 Sawmill Road
Suite 304
Dublin, Ohio 43016
http://www.telemachuspress.com

ISBN: 978-1-956867-83-1 (eBook)
ISBN: 978-1-956867-84-8 (Paperback)

Library of Congress Control Number: 2023923178

Version 2023.12.04

Table of Contents

I. A Most Welcome Guest 1

II. The Baal Shem Tov's Magical Journey 4

III. The Hidden Saint Learns of His Mission 9

IV. Tzedakah 21

V. To Cleanse Through Shame 26

VI. A New Life 37

VII. When Dreams Come True 40

VIII. The Fall 47

IX. A Hidden Saint's Days of Righteousness 54

X. The Death of the Hidden Saint 59

XI. The Nobleman's Tale 64

Other Books by Barak Bassman 77

The Twisted Path of the Hidden Saint:
An Occult Tale of the Baal Shem Tov

I. A Most Welcome Guest

REB SHLOMO, THE innkeeper in the *shtetl* of Z, had been sweltering for hours in the heavy late summer heat. At last, however, the air cooled as twilight fell and his tavern, which had been empty all day, now quickly filled with Jews and Poles looking to slake their thirst and rest their legs after laboring hard beneath the boiling sun.

As he was merrily hopping from table to table, filling cups and serving pickled herring and onions and bread, Reb Shlomo spied a man entering his tavern whom he remembered well—a wanderer who told the most marvelous tales, tales that quickened the pulse and exalted the soul and ended with a rich serving of true Torah wisdom. Shlomo put his tray down and shouted out to the crowded room to quiet down, for he had something important to tell them. My esteemed friends and guests, he said, tonight we have been truly blessed. Standing here—and he pointed at the man who had just walked in—is Reb Jacob from the *shtetl* of Mezhbizh. For many years, Reb Jacob was a disciple of Rabbi Israel ben Eliezer, the holy Baal Shem Tov, may the memory of the righteous be for a blessing and may their merit protect us. And when the Baal Shem Tov was on his deathbed, he commanded Reb Jacob to pick up his staff, travel to wherever Jews can be found, and earn his living telling tales—true tales—of the wondrous and miraculous deeds of the

Baal Shem Tov. Reb Jacob has passed through this tavern several times before, and the tales he told of his great *tzaddik* have elevated my soul and the soul of every other man fortunate enough to hear them. So, come, everybody now, sit with us and listen. I will bring Reb Jacob his favorite Hungarian wine—nothing but the best for my old friend—and we shall hear some tales this evening that will show us the true path of righteousness and Torah.

He led Reb Jacob to a table exactly in the middle of the room, and all the other patrons gathered around in a circle. Shlomo dashed off to his cellar to fill a large pitcher of Tokay, ran back up to the kitchen to grab a plate piled high with freshly baked honey cakes, and then set this sweet repast before his honored guest. Reb Jacob kindly thanked Shlomo for his gracious hospitality, recited two quick blessings, and plunged with gusto into his food and drink.

A Pole stepped forward from the crowd and approached Reb Jacob. This man was elegantly dressed, and appeared to Shlomo to be a wealthy nobleman, although not someone whom Shlomo recognized as a resident of that district—another traveler, the innkeeper supposed.

The nobleman addressed Reb Jacob in fluent Yiddish: Good sir, I am delighted to make your acquaintance. I have heard from many Jews about the holiness and wisdom of your late master, the Baal Shem Tov—his death was a terrible tragedy for your people. If our host the innkeeper does not object, I have a request for a particular tale, for which I will pay you handsomely. The Jews who live on my lands tell me that there are thirty-six hidden saints in each generation. But for the merits of these thirty-six men, my Jews say to me, God would destroy the world again in another flood, and this time he might not even find a Noah worth saving. Tell me, Reb Jacob, did your master and teacher ever meet such a hidden saint? What tales can you tell us of these hidden saints?

Reb Shlomo felt his heart swell at these words and he shouted out: Your Honor makes a wonderful suggestion. Yes, Reb Jacob, tell us a tale of the Baal Shem Tov and one of the *lamed-vovniks*, the thirty-six hidden saints who sustain the world by their righteousness.

Reb Jacob frowned and opened his mouth as if he was about to say something but then stopped, sighed and stared down into his empty cup. After a brief moment of silence, he lifted his head and spoke: I can tell you the tale of when the Baal Shem Tov met a hidden saint. I was there and I remember what happened. But I must warn you, this tale is not simple or joyous. It is filled with mysteries that can cloud even a righteous man's clear sight. Perhaps you would prefer some lighter fare to feast on tonight? This strangely spiced dish might upset your stomach.

Reb Shlomo replied that he would defer to the wishes of his noble guest. The *Pan*, in turn, repeated that he wished to hear the tale of the hidden saint and nothing else and stressed again that he would pay quite well—and he named a figure.

The other Jews and Poles audibly gasped at the size of this number.

Reb Jacob then said that, since His Lordship insisted, he would tell the tale.

II. The Baal Shem Tov's Magical Journey

REB JACOB SLOUCHED back in his chair and launched into his tale: My dear friends, the events that I will relate to you tonight, as wondrous as they may seem, were all true—I only tell you what my eyes saw and what my ears heard. It happened many years ago, on a summer night much like this one. Back then, I was so young—not even one grey hair in my beard. And my master and teacher, the holy *tzaddik*, the light of our exile, the pillar of his generation, may his merit protect us, Rabbi Israel ben Eliezer, the righteous Baal Shem Tov, was still alive and in this world, walking about like you and me. Back then, all those years ago, I lived in Mezhbizh, in the house of the Baal Shem Tov. I was his disciple, and sometimes his scribe and his attendant.

On that particular summer day, the Baal Shem Tov had been strangely preoccupied. From the moment he awoke, he was unable to concentrate upon his prayers or his studies. When Jews came knocking at the door seeking his help—to cure a child's illness, to open a woman's barren womb—he told me to send them away and ask that they return again in a few days' time.

Why, I asked, can my master not come to the aid of Jews in need? What worry can be weighing so terribly on his heart?

But he would not answer me.

All through the morning, the Baal Shem Tov paced about his study, mumbling to himself. He stubbornly refused all offers of food and drink. Then, at noon, he stormed out of the house towards the forest. When I tried to follow, he ordered me to remain behind.

I asked his Chana of blessed memory if she knew what was troubling her husband. But she only shrugged and sighed and shook her head. I suppose that, being the wife of a great *tzaddik* whose soul would often ascend to higher worlds, she had become accustomed to her husband wandering off and doing mysterious things.

The Baal Shem Tov returned around twilight. He told me to fetch his coachman and round up his horses, for we had an urgent journey to make that evening.

Where are we going? I asked.

A man is dying, the Baal Shem Tov replied, and I wish to see him and learn his wisdom before his soul departs from this world. I want you to come with me, so that you can also hear what he may have to say. Now, go quickly, his light is fading fast and time is short.

I ran at once straight from my master to the inn in Mezhbizh, where the Baal Shem Tov stabled his horses. I found our coachman there on the porch of the tavern, sprawled out on a bench, stinking of vodka. I smacked him on the cheeks a couple of times to rouse him from his stupor, and then I said that the master needed to leave on a journey and there was no time to waste.

Stepan the coachman stood up slowly, bent over, vomited up the liquor he had drunk—and nearly right onto my shoes, mind you—and went over to the stables. He hitched the horses to the wagon, and we both got in and drove back over to the house of the Baal Shem Tov. The *tzaddik* hopped in next to me in the back, and we were off.

The horses proceeded at a comfortable trot until we left the town. Then the Baal Shem Tov pointed his finger at Stepan and loudly recited combinations of the secret names of different angels. The coachman immediately let go of the reins, turned around in his seat, and fell asleep. In less than a minute, he was snoring loudly.

The horses now went faster, much faster. Soon they were going so fast that they leapt off the ground and we were flying up, high above the treetops, close to the clouds. We soared through the night sky, swifter than the feeble birds who could not keep up with us.

I peeked over the edge of the wagon and saw that everything down below looked so tiny now, as if the houses and trees and barns had been turned into little wooden toys for children. Scared I would fall to my death, I flung myself onto the floor in the middle of the wagon, curled up into a tight ball, and shut my eyes.

But then I heard beautiful singing that calmed my nerves and lifted my spirits. I slowly opened one eye. And what did that one eye see? The Baal Shem Tov smiling and singing and waving to the birds as we passed them in the air. He did not seem to have a care in the world.

Still, I went back to shutting my eyes—even the sight of my master's joy could not release me from the terror of falling that had gripped my heart.

After a while, I felt a thud and the horses slackened their pace. I lifted my head and saw that we were once more on the ground. The coachman had woken up and was holding the reins. We were in a forest somewhere, on a poorly paved road full of weeds. I did not see a village or a town anywhere, or even a barn.

I looked over at the Baal Shem Tov, who seemed lost in his own thoughts. I almost asked him where we were going, but then I reminded myself that wherever we were, we had not arrived by natural means. Something great and wondrous was afoot, and it was not my place to question the mysterious acts of the *tzaddik*.

Eventually we stopped in a clearing. In the bright moonlight, I could make out a small hut, but it did not look like anyone lived there—there were huge holes in the roof that would let the rain and wind pummel whomever might be foolish enough to step inside. I figured that it had to be a long abandoned ruin.

But then the Baal Shem Tov told me that the wise, learned sage whom he was seeking—the one who was about to die—was inside that wreck of a hut. Although I could not imagine how any person, much less a great sage, would want to live in a hut with a roof full of holes surrounded by nothing but trees and wolves, I did not argue. I told myself to trust in my master, the *tzaddik*. This was clearly no ordinary night, and whoever awaited us in that hut was not going to be an ordinary man.

When we entered, I saw that there was a weak fire in a pit on the floor casting off a dull orange glow. Between that light and the moonbeams pouring in through the holes in the roof, we were able to see quite clearly. Not that there was much to see: Aside from the fire, there was only a pitcher of water, an empty cup, and a bowl with a few crumbs in it.

And there was also a man lying on the ground—the man whom we had come all this way to see and hear. His beard and hair were white as a shroud and had grown long and wild, like weeds sprouting all over his head. His body was shriveled and starved to the bone. There were sores and boils on his skin, his lips, and even one of his eyes, which he could barely keep open. He trembled underneath a blanket too moth-eaten and short to give him much comfort.

Even though he saw us enter his hut, the man neither stirred nor spoke. It was as if we were merely two blades of grass that the wind had blown past his threshold.

The Baal Shem Tov sat down next to this wretched man and signaled to me to do the same. Then he said: Holy *tzaddik*, master and teacher, I am Reb Israel ben Eliezer. I have heard of your great righteousness. Please, tonight, unburden your heart and teach me the secrets and wisdom you have learned.

But in response, the man only made this gurgling noise—and here Reb Jacob paused to imitate the sound for his audience in the tavern—like a frog choking on a chicken bone.

The Baal Shem Tov sighed with pity at the man's suffering and then, with his eyes narrowed in intense concentration, he recited a series of combinations of secret and potent true names for the Holy One, Blessed be He. When he was finished, he said in plain Yiddish again: Holy master, please try speaking now.

And the man said: But I am too ill to speak.

The Baal Shem Tov answered him: Yet now you can speak again.

How is this possible? the man replied. How can you work such miracles?

The Baal Shem Tov said he did not work miracles, but only harnessed and released the divine sparks already within the souls around him.

The man spoke some more now: Since you have restored my voice to me, what do you wish for me to say? My days in this hut are all alike, filled to the brim with tedium and misery.

In that case, the Baal Shem Tov said, tell me about your days before you came to this hut.

The man let out a loud, anguished sigh. That was long ago, he said. But if you have come all this way, and gone to the trouble of restoring my voice, I will tell you what you wish to know.

III. The Hidden Saint Learns of His Mission

REB JACOB STRETCHED his limbs and let out a yawn. Shlomo the innkeeper poured some more wine into his cup and urged him to continue. After glancing around again at the eager, silent faces to his right and to his left, Reb Jacob continued:

So, the man in the hut agreed to tell us his tale. And as I remember, this is what he said: I was born in the *shtetl* of K. in White Russia. My father of blessed memory was a wealthy man. For many years, he held the leasehold rights to several distilleries on the estate of a certain nobleman. He also dabbled in other bits of business here and there, some wine barrels, some furs, some timber.

I was the youngest of four sons, the surprise blessing of my parents' old age. As my brothers were much older than me, by the time I could walk, they had all married and moved far away. My father was also often away tending to his business affairs. My mother was a kind woman, but very quiet and easily upset. She was short and slight and her old, stiff bones wobbled uneasily under the weight of her heavy matron's wig. She would silently drift into the corners of rooms and, like a mouse, burrow into hidden crevices where you could no longer see her. When I tried to play with her, she would recoil in terror and call desperately for the servants to take me away.

My one friend, or at least companion, was my tutor. My father did not trust the greasy *melamed* who ran the town's *cheder* in a dark basement packed with screaming, brawling brats. My older brothers had also been taught by private tutors until they were old enough to study in a *yeshiva*, but at least they had each other for company. I envied the loud, dirty boys who got to spend their days together in that damp basement classroom. On *Shabbat*, I would sometimes try to talk to them, but I could not follow their gossip about what had happened in the *cheder* that past week. And I was terrible at the games they played with each other—I had unfortunately inherited my mother's frail constitution. So, like my mother, I silently drifted into the cracks in the walls.

My tutor, though, was an excellent teacher. He first taught me *chumash* with Rashi's commentary, then the other books of the *Tanakh*, Midrash, Talmud, and all their commentaries. These holy books filled my head with yearning and dreams. I longed to embrace the prophets and kings of Judah and Israel. In my mind, I walked with the holy sages of blessed memory and stood with Rabbi Akiva in defiance against the wicked Romans. I wept when they burned him alive as he cried out the *shema* prayer with his last breath.

Yet however lonely and sorrowful I may have been, day still followed day and eventually I grew old enough to study at the *yeshiva* in our town. And then I was happy, at long last, for I quickly became friends with the other boys studying there. As some of them had traveled to the *yeshiva* from faraway and had no relatives nearby, I convinced my parents to let them eat at our table. One even slept in our house. We would argue about the correct interpretation of passages in the Talmud all through the day and all through the night. And I did not care if I won or lost these arguments. I just felt such joy to be with true friends who greeted me each morning with a warm smile and included me in their gossip and petty feuds.

I did not want these precious days to end. I was scared that if I married and left the *yeshiva*, I would be forced to return to my earlier loneliness—a loneliness made even more bitter by the brief, sweet taste of genuine friendship. And so, I found many excuses to avoid meeting with girls who were potential brides. If I had to meet them, then I would seize upon any pretext to reject the match: This one was a fool who could not be trusted to run a household; that one was not pretty enough; and this other girl had seemed too cold and distracted to make a good mother to my children.

My father was furious. He would say to me: Do you think you are going to find a bride who is more beautiful than Queen Esther, wiser than the Queen of Sheba, and more loyal and devoted than Rabbi Akiva's wife? Do you actually think such a girl could even exist?

But I would reply that I was only trying to make sure I made a good match that would not end in a shameful divorce. My father would then throw his arms up in the air and ask *HaShem* why he had been cursed to have such a stubborn fool of a son.

Yet regardless of my wishes, time moved on. My friends in the *yeshiva* slowly drifted away, one by one, as they married and moved into their new fathers-in-laws' distant homes. The new boys, the younger boys, formed their own friendships. One day, the *rosh* (principal) of the *yeshiva* finally pulled me aside and said it was long past time for me to take a wife and fulfill the commandment to have children and carry on the generations of Israel. And so, with a heavy heart, I resigned myself to my fate and agreed to the next match that my father proposed.

I went to live with my new father-in-law, who lived about a three days' wagon ride from the town where I was born. He was a wine merchant and planned to bring me into his business. However, as I was considered to be a scholar, my father had bargained in the engagement contract for three years of board while I continued my studies in the town's *bet midrash*.

My married life was dull and wearying. I studied all day, but without friends to debate and argue with the words of the holy sages remained dead on the dusty pages. The two or three other young husbands who also came to the *bet midrash* each day had little interest in their studies and mostly gossiped with each other about their future plans for opening this or that business.

My wife was neither pleasing nor displeasing to me. We had a few children, little boys. She devoted all her thoughts and attentions to their needs, but I did not feel jealous or slighted, as this was what she was supposed to be doing with her days as a young mother.

And what was I supposed to be doing? I was supposed to be studying, but the words of the holy books now bored me. I was also supposed to be thinking about joining my father-in-law's wine business. I thought about how I would travel with him to Hungary to buy wine barrels, haul them back to White Russia, and then sell our fine merchandise to noblemen and bishops and monasteries. I tried to imagine what this would be like. My father-in-law was a good man, but the only matter he enjoyed discussing was his business. My future days would be spent with this man, in wagons and carriages, in taverns and inns, speaking of nothing but grapes and barrels and vintages and prices. He did not even take any pleasure in drinking the wine, the way his wealthy customers did. His joy was only in the buying and the selling.

I was filled with despair at the thought of being tossed between my father-in-law's tedious discussions of wine prices and the complaints of my wife exhausted from being grabbed at and cried at by our children. Yet what else was I to do?

But then one day, shortly before Passover, something extraordinary happened. I was sitting alone in the *bet midrash* at twilight. As I could not muster the strength to stare any longer at the books spread out before me, I lifted my eyes to the window and gazed at the pink clouds. A tremendous weariness suddenly overcame me and I quickly fell into a deep sleep.

In my dream, the most wondrous vision appeared to me. I was walking in a wide meadow with tall grass. The air was warm but not too warm, and above my head there was a clear blue sky. I strode forward until I came upon a large manor house, such as a rich nobleman would live in.

I saw a tall woman standing on the porch, garbed in the kind of immodest dress that Polish countesses wear. She had thick black hair that fell down to her waist and gleaming black eyes, almost like a cat. Her face was pretty, but not young. There was something harsh about her expression, as if she were upset with someone. Still, when she saw me approach, she smiled, greeted me by my name, and invited me to join her inside.

We entered the house and went into a parlor room with wide bay windows. The floor and the fireplace were fashioned from white and blue marble. The ceiling was decorated with paintings of pink skies and white clouds and almost naked men and women chasing one another and laughing and blushing.

I sat down on a couch next to this woman, close to her but not touching. She told me that I had been tasked with a special and important mission from the Heavenly Court. But she was not sure if I was ready to do what I must do.

And then, before I could say anything, she asked me, without warning or explanation, a series of questions about the ethical teachings of our holy sages of blessed memory set forth in the *Pirkei Avot*. But as I had never studied that tractate closely, my answers were fumbling and foolish.

After a while, she stopped testing me with her questions, stood up, and told me I was not yet ready. I had to learn the importance of ethics, of charity and righteousness, and not merely how to argue abstruse points of the law. She said that I would not be permitted to return to her presence until I had thoroughly learned the *Pirkei Avot*.

And then I awoke. As the sun had set while I had been napping, I left the *bet midrash* and hurried home to eat dinner with my family.

While I found this dream to be strange and mysterious, I assumed at the time that it was just that—some dream, which I would quickly forget.

Yet over the next several days, I kept thinking of that dream. I felt ashamed of my ignorance before that noblewoman, even though I reminded myself that she was only a figment of my imagination. And how could she be anything else? Whoever heard of a Polish countess being so passionately devoted to the teachings of the *Pirkei Avot*? What would her priest say?

Nevertheless, I could not summon her back again in my dreams, no matter how hard I tried. This struck me as odd: As I had invented this countess in my mind, I should be able to conjure her apparition whenever I pleased. Yet, although I yearned to have another look at her, when my eyelids closed, she simply would not obey my command to appear.

Eventually, I resolved to do as she had asked and studied the *Pirkei Avot* to see if that would compel her to return to my dreams. I pulled the tractate off the shelf in the *bet midrash* and dove into it, swaying over the book from dawn to dusk for several days in a row and sticking my nose into every commentary that I could find. I let my soul marinate in these ancient teachings about humility and charity and loving kindness.

And then she came back to me. It was on a Saturday afternoon, just after I had eaten. I leaned back in the soft, upholstered chair, my stomach as heavy as a boulder, and let the *Shabbes* afternoon nap carry me away. Soon I could feel myself snoring loudly and breathing heavily. I heard my wife scolding my sons about who knows what, but she sounded so distant she might as well have been in Jerusalem.

I started to dream. There was a blue sky with puffy white clouds. I glanced at my feet and saw that I was standing in a meadow of tall grass. I looked up again and there was the manor house from my earlier dream, just as I had remembered it. And on the porch of that manor house I saw her, the same noblewoman in her immodest dress, standing erect and staring straight at me. When our eyes met, she greeted me by name and invited me to join her inside.

I followed her into the same parlor room with the bay windows. We sat down together on the couch. She said she was pleased that I had finally turned my studies toward their proper purpose. However, she wanted to be sure that I had fully mastered the lessons that I needed to learn and thus she wished to test me once more.

In response, I nodded my head and said I was ready.

Good, she said. And then she asked question after question about this or that passage in the *Pirkei Avot*. This time I was able to answer all of them with ease. The noble lady smiled and praised me for my diligence and scholarship.

When she was finished, she asked me: Have you ever studied the teaching given in the name of Abbaye of blessed memory, that there are not less than thirty-six righteous men in each generation who greet the Divine Presence?

I said that I was familiar with this teaching.

And what does it mean? she asked.

I laughed and said to her: Every child knows what it means. In every generation, there are thirty-six hidden saints—the *lamed-vovniks*—for the sake of whose righteousness the Holy One, Blessed be He, permits the world to continue to exist. Otherwise, in His just rage at our many sins, He would destroy the world with another great flood.

She pressed on: And do you believe with perfect faith that these *lamed-vovniks* walk in your midst and that their work, their mission, is what permits you to live? Not just you, but everyone around you, everyone living and breathing in this world?

I shrugged and said how should I know—*lamed-vovniks* are hidden saints. If they were walking about in my midst, then they would be hidden from me.

Do you think, she replied, that the *lamed-vovniks* know that they are hidden saints?

How would they know? I said. It is not as if the prophet Samuel anoints their heads with oil.

But then she jumped up from the couch, extended her long forefinger at me, and shouted: The fate of the world rests on the shoulders of the *lamed-vovniks*. If they do not know their mission, then how can they perform it? What if they should be tempted, by pride, lust, greed, envy? The very existence of this world could be imperiled.

I was beginning to wonder if I was trapped with a madwoman. I decided it was time for this dream to end. But I could not wake myself. Nor could I make this vision go away so that I could dream about something else—something more pleasant. It was as if some evil spirit had taken possession of my mind.

As I could not escape, I tried to calm her: I said that a true *lamed-vovnik* was so full of love for *HaShem* that he would think only of prayer and charity.

But she screamed back at me: Lies, you speak lies! All men are prey to temptation—you are all the children of Adam and Eve, who spurned the commandment of the Holy One, Blessed be He, and were enticed by the serpent. Every *lamed-vovnik* is tempted. He can only resist the lure of sin because he knows how great his mission is.

In reply, I asked her: How can a *lamed-vovnik* know he is a hidden saint? Any man who thinks he is a hidden saint upon whom the world's fate depends is no doubt so puffed up with pride and arrogance that he lacks the humility of a true *lamed-vovnik*. To be arrogant enough to think you are a *lamed-vovnik* is proof that you cannot be one.

And then I suddenly woke up.

I concluded that this noblewoman—whether a spirit haunting me or a figment of my imagination—was completely mad and it was best to avoid her company in the future. And so, I stopped studying the *Pirkei Avot*, in the hope that this would dissuade her from appearing again in my dreams.

In fact, I ceased my studies of the Talmud altogether. I was worried that I had spent so much time away from the world with these books that my mind was losing its grip on reality and thus bombarding me with these wild feverish dreams.

I asked my father-in-law to teach me about his business. I was done with studying all day, I said to him. It was time for me to become a man who knew how to carry on a trade and support his family.

He replied: Are you sure you want to give up your studies so soon? You do not need to—*Baruch HaShem*, my business has prospered and there is plenty of money for food and drink for everyone.

I replied: The wheel of fortune can turn suddenly and without warning. What if, Heaven forbid, you became ill? Or your carriage had an accident on the road? Who then would provide for our family? I am not a boy anymore. I am a husband and a father, and it is my responsibility to provide for the household should anything befall you.

My father-in-law nodded gravely. He said that he understood and would teach me his business.

Over the next few weeks, my father-in-law the wine merchant instructed me in the many varieties of wines he sold and where and how the grapes were grown. As his inventory was well-stocked at the time, we did not need yet to travel back to the vineyards in Hungary that supplied our barrels. But we did make many trips together to call upon his customers—to noblemen's estates and monasteries and cathedrals and wealthy merchants. My father-in-law was right—business was good.

And when we were not meeting with customers and taking down their orders, we were arranging for the shipment of our barrels from the warehouse and balancing the ledgers and accounts. I even lifted and rolled some of the barrels myself, which was no easy task for a pampered *yeshiva bochur*.

By the time we had finished our work and *davened* our evening prayers, I was exhausted. I would collapse into a comfortable chair while my little sons played with each other at my feet. My wife would bring me a glass of brandy and a slice of honey cake. I noticed that she looked upon me with a newfound respect. I was not a boy any longer, nitpicking with the other boys over what the *Gemara* said about how grain offerings were once made in the Temple in Jerusalem. No, I was a man, shouldering the responsibility of providing sustenance for my family. She even became quite eager to lie with me—something that she had done before only on Friday nights, and even then, with a stifled sigh of impatience and irritation. I wondered why I had ever dreaded entering the wine business. I thought: This is how I was meant to live. To be a prosperous merchant, a shrewd man of business, with a devoted wife and many children.

But then one night, in my dream, I found myself standing again in that same broad, grassy meadow—the very place I had hoped to avoid by abandoning my studies. This time, though, the sky was dark, rain poured down furiously upon my head, and thunder boomed in my ears.

I ran to the porch of the manor house, where at least the roof would protect me from the storm. Fortunately, I did not see the mad Polish noblewoman there. And even though the door to the house was open, I did not go inside.

As this was a dream, I cannot tell you how much time passed while I sat on that porch. However, after a while I felt several large, firm hands seize me and hoist me up in the air. But when I looked around, I did not see anyone there, just floating clouds of barely visible black mist. These black clouds carried me inside the house, placed me down upon the couch in the parlor room, and then disappeared.

A fire now suddenly kindled in the hearth and the chandelier above my head was instantly illuminated with its many candles.

I shielded my eyes from the painful brightness.

When I looked up again, I saw *her*—that strange, mad noblewoman who apparently lived in this place. She was seated next to me on the couch, wearing a long black dress with a thin black veil. She sighed loudly, almost angrily.

I said nothing in response. I hoped she would just leave and then I could wake up and get back to my pleasant life as a budding wine merchant.

However, rather than leave, she spoke to me: You are bringing the wrath of the Heavenly Court down upon your head. You have a great mission, a wondrous mission, to fulfill in this world. And yet you waste your allotted portion of days on childish trifles—all your silly haggling over barrels of wine.

But I said back to her: *Nu*, tell me, what is this great mission? I am just an ordinary Jew trying to make a living and feed my children. And what is so wrong with that? Why must you keep berating me in my dreams? Leave me alone and let me dream of something else.

The noblewoman let out another sigh, even louder than the first, and she slowly shook her head at me. She said: How can you be such a blind fool? You are bringing ruin upon yourself, upon the entire world, and yet you still claim to be just an ordinary Jew. You know what you must do. So why won't you do it?

By this point, I desperately wanted to wake up and make her vanish from my sight, but try as I might, I was stuck in this dream. So, in my frustration, I yelled at her: What is this crazy nonsense that you keep babbling about? Either tell me what this so-called mission is in plain simple Yiddish or go away.

She answered me in a voice that was surprisingly calm, almost tender: You truly cannot grasp the truth of these matters? Then I will reveal what you fail to understand, for otherwise you will continue to go astray and there may be grave consequences. As you wish, in plain simple Yiddish: You are a *lamed-vovnik*, a hidden saint, one of the thirty-six righteous men for whose sake the world is permitted to continue to exist. You must devote yourself to charity and good deeds, not to dealing in wine barrels.

And then I suddenly woke up.

IV. *Tzedakah*

THE NEXT MORNING, I laughed at my wild dream. How could I be a hidden saint, a *lamed-vovnik*? Hidden saints are sickly, starving wretches so oppressed by their poverty, so humble and quiet, that they are not even noticed by those around them—and yet their souls are so filled with love of *HaShem* that they devote their days to extraordinary, but secret, acts of charity and prayer. I, on the other hand, was the spoiled son-in-law of a wealthy merchant whose table was always piled high with warm, fresh delicacies. So how could I be a *lamed-vovnik*? The notion was absurd.

But then I started to wonder why I had dreamed something so strange. Was there any truth in it somewhere? Certainly, I was no hidden saint, but perhaps I had not been as attentive to charity and prayer as I should have been. Although I prayed when I was supposed to, I rushed through my prayers and did not pay close attention to the Hebrew words in the *siddur*. I was sure that, in my haste, I must have stumbled over many phrases.

And so, I resolved to slow down and concentrate more closely on my prayers. At the synagogue that morning, I sat down alone on a bench in a distant back corner and forced myself to focus hard on each and every word of each and every prayer. By the time I was finished, the synagogue was empty and the *shammes* was scowling at me for lingering so long. But I paid him no mind.

When I finally arrived at the warehouse, my father-in-law rebuked me for being so late and asked if I had overslept. When I told him that I had decided to meditate upon each word in my morning prayers, to savor tenderly each praise of the Holy One, Blessed be He, in all His Infinite Power and Goodness, my father-in-law merely sighed and shook his head.

But regardless of my father-in-law's disapproval, my heart was full of joy. I recited my evening prayers with even greater slow concentration. When I came home, much later than usual because I had lingered so long in the synagogue, my wife told me that everyone else had already eaten and she had nothing left for me but cold potato soup and pickled herring. Although my belly growled and ached, I recalled the many nights I had rushed through my prayers to dash home to wet my lips with warm, moist delicacies. Desiring to atone for these past sins, I said I was not hungry.

I went to bed early that evening, as I was weak from hunger. I dreamed that night of a beautiful white doe, with big sad eyes, running through a forest to escape from a pack of vicious, drooling black wolves. The doe ran to me and jumped in my arms, begging for my protection.

My eyes then suddenly opened. It was midnight. I understood immediately what this dream meant: The white doe was the *Shekhinah*, the Divine Presence suffering in exile, and the black wolves were the demons of the *sitra achra*, the forces of wickedness. I left my bed, lit a candle, and went down to the kitchen. There, I sat at the table with my *siddur* and chanted Psalms until sleep overcame me once more.

This became the new way that I spent my days: in prayer, morning, afternoon, evening, and midnight, lingering and concentrating lovingly upon each word. I neglected my father-in-law's wine business, but I did not care so much anymore about such earthly trifles.

I ate less and less, just barely enough to keep my body and soul stitched together. Two days a week I fasted completely so that I could offer up my withering flesh as an atonement sacrifice to the Holy One, Blessed be He, for the years in which I had been lax in my devotions to Him—true devotions, and not merely the motions of idle Torah study. As my body shriveled from hunger, my soul was lighter and freer, and I felt myself less bound to this lowly material world.

And then another thought occurred to me: What should be done with the food that I formerly used to eat? It was not as if my wife or in-laws or children had suddenly started eating more to make up for my fasting. Would it not be pleasing to *HaShem* if we engaged in the *mitzvah* of hospitality and brought the poor to our table?

So, after my evening prayers one night, I asked the *shammes* to take me to the room in the back of the synagogue where wandering beggars were permitted to sleep so they could at least have a roof over their heads. He looked at me strangely, no doubt wondering what I could want with a pack of smelly, pushy beggars, but then he shrugged his shoulders and led me to them.

The room was dark—the only light came from the fading sunset filtering through a small, high window. And the stink was terrible—I am sure none of these men had washed in weeks. The beggars were a hideous sight, puss-oozing boils and peeling scabs and rashes all over their skin. One of them was missing a leg, another was missing an ear. In their eyes there was such sorrow and loneliness and despair. These were men who had given up on the love and mercy of the Holy One, Blessed be He.

You can imagine their surprise when I told them that they were going to dine at my table. The *shammes* asked me if I had misspoken—did I really intend to bring *all* of them back to my house? But I insisted that was exactly what I had meant, and so they came away with me.

My wife and mother-in-law were aghast when they beheld the troop of beggars and tried to drive them away. But I held firm, and I sternly reminded them of the words of King Solomon, may his merit protect us: *Charity saves from death*. And then they quieted their complaints and served the beggars from their own more than ample portions.

Over the next several weeks, I invited more and more beggars to eat at our table. I also paid for candles to be lit in the beggars' room in the back of the synagogue and for wood to heat their stove. I hired tailors to mend their clothes, cobblers to give them proper shoes, and doctors to tend to their wounds. I insisted that they accompany me to the *mikveh* to bathe their bodies properly, and I did not let the attendant there show them any dishonor.

After a while, my father-in-law had had enough of all this *tzedekah*. He pulled me aside and said: What is wrong with you? Why are all my profits going into the pockets of good-for-nothing beggars? How has it become my responsibility alone to feed and clothe the poor? You idiot, don't you realize that the community takes care of them? We householders each give a little bit of money—but not too much—into a common fund, and then the *shammes* uses that fund as needed for the upkeep of the poor. What is so wrong with that? I contribute my share, like any good Jew, but I never turned my household upside down. Do you think your wife enjoys the company of beggars? Have you noticed how they leer at her bosom and snicker?

But I would not budge. I calmly, but firmly, reminded my father-in-law that this life is but a brief flicker, a quick passing illusion, and that our eternal souls would soon be hauled before the Heavenly Tribunal for judgment. Through our acts of charity, we atone for our many sins. Did he expect to merit a portion in the

World to Come by squeezing a few more zlotys of profit from some drunken Polish count?

In response, my father-in-law threw his hands up in the air and asked his Creator what terrible sin he had committed to be afflicted with such a crazy blockhead for a son-in-law.

Still, while my father-in-law might have cursed me, the other Jews in the town hailed me as a great *tzaddik*, a holy saint. Tales of my devotion to prayer and charity spread far and wide. Jews from faraway towns traveled to my *shtetl* to seek my blessing. Young men from wealthy families, students at the finest *yeshivot* in Poland and Lithuania, came to me and begged me to teach them my Torah—for they too had heard of my righteous ways and wished to walk in my path.

V. To Cleanse Through Shame

BY THIS TIME, it had been many months since I had last dreamed of the noblewoman and her manor house. But then one night, I dreamt again that I was standing in that same meadow. While the sky was blue and calm at first, it quickly darkened, and hail rained down. The hard ice struck my forehead and blood rushed down my face, pouring into my eyes and mouth.

Full of terror, I ran towards the manor house, onto the porch, and through the open front door into the parlor room. There, everything was in disarray—the furniture was overturned and broken and strewn about the floor, and the marble floors and mantelpiece were covered in streaks of thick black grime.

When the noblewoman entered the room, she also looked wretched: Her hair was wild and disheveled, her elegant dress was torn in several places, and she had dark swollen bags under her eyes, as if she had not slept for many days.

Staggering toward me, with her long, bony finger pointed at my head, she said: Disgusting, horrible sinner, filth, dog, worm, maggot, you have brought the wrath of the Holy One, Blessed be He, down upon both of our heads. We must atone—*you* must atone. Your wickedness has set the angels of the Heavenly Tribunal to work crafting terrible decrees of retribution—upon you, upon your family, upon all Israel. You stand on the edge of the cliff, and your feet are slipping. Soon your fragile bones will shatter against the jagged rocks, and then the wolves will find your crippled body in the gorge and feast slowly upon what is left of you.

Repent now, while you still can. You are fortunate the Throne of Glory permitted me to come to you again to try once more to rescue your putrid soul.

Her words bewildered me. What terrible sin had I committed? Every Jew in Poland and Lithuania had been hailing me as a saint and praising me for my works of charity. And hadn't this very same woman insisted that I was a hidden saint, a *lamed-vovnik*? Why should she be angry with me for devoting myself to the care of the poor?

And so, when she had finally finished yelling at me, I answered her with these words: How can you rebuke me for being a terrible sinner who must urgently repent? I devote all my days to charity and prayer. *You* told me I was a *lamed-vovnik*. *You* persuaded me to ignore vain studies and worldly pursuits. And now you reproach me for doing exactly what you had asked for—leading a life devoted to simple piety and *mitzvot*?

In response, the noble lady threw her hands up in the air and shrieked with rage, like a wild animal with its tail caught in a snare. Then she spoke again: You arrogant fool, you *are* a hidden saint— and you have betrayed your mission so grievously that even the prayers of all the other hidden saints are not enough to appease the wrath of the Heavenly Tribunal. The world is sustained by the thirty-six righteous pillars of each generation precisely because their righteousness is concealed from everyone else in this base, lowly world. Their good deeds flow from the purest source: not any yearning for fame or adulation, but only love for *HaShem* and His Torah.

You have flaunted your *mitzvot* wantonly, seeking the praises of your fellow men. How can the Holy One, Blessed be He, trust that your righteous deeds flow from a pure source? Perhaps you are doing them only for your own pride?

Now it was my turn to throw my hands up in the air and sigh loudly with frustration. And then I said back to her: This is absurd. I am having a dream. You are not real. This place is not real. That hailstorm is not real. I am going to wake up any minute, in my own bed, in my own house. And then you will be gone. Whoever you are, phantom, demon, your words make no sense. Am I a sinner because I have performed too many good deeds? And how am I supposed to atone for giving too much charity—by committing crimes and transgressions? By robbing a beggar?

She replied: So then, you refuse to change your ways? You will not heed my words?

By this point, I had lost my patience and I shouted back at her: No, I will not heed your ridiculous stupid words!

She then said, in a calm voice: If that is your choice, so be it. You will be tested. And when the test is upon you, and you are ready to listen, I shall return to you once more.

And then I woke up.

I felt uneasy for the rest of the day, as if something terrible lurked behind every corner and was about to pounce upon me and tear me limb from limb. But later that night, when nothing had happened, I rebuked myself for being so foolish as to be frightened by a dream. After all, what is a dream? A silly apparition conjured up by my own mind to scare me.

For the next several days, I went about my rounds of prayer and charity as usual. I tried to forget the noblewoman and her manor house and her threats.

But then my eldest son, who was still just a small boy, fell ill. His body burned with fever and his skin broke out in rashes and boils. He coughed and he wheezed, and he spit up thick green mucus that splattered all over his mouth and cheeks. Everything that he ate came back up in a heap of warm vomit.

My father-in-law immediately sent for the most esteemed physicians in the district—no expense was spared for his beloved grandson. These learned doctors examined the patient, consulted with each other, debated etiologies and diagnoses, and eventually prescribed all sorts of foul-smelling, strange-colored medicines.

But none of it made any difference. His condition only grew worse.

The town's rabbi ordered a fast day and recited Psalms for the boy's recovery, but again all of this was to no avail. My mother-in-law brought in Polish wise women, witch healers, who rubbed their herbs deep into the boy's diseased skin and screamed out their incantations, but these too accomplished nothing.

Finally, the town's rabbi sent for a *baal shem*, a Jew deeply learned in the practical *kabbalah*, to wield the power of secret holy names to heal my son and drive away the demons that were tormenting his body. This *baal shem* spent a night alone with my son, praying fervently and reciting his formulas.

The next morning, the *baal shem* pulled me aside. He said: I know you are a righteous man, renowned for your piety and your charity. And yet when I summoned the angels to heal your child, they did not come. I struggled for hours for my pleas to be heard in the Heavenly Tribunal, but it was no use.

And then a woman's voice—a voice I did not recognize—whispered to me: This child suffers on account of his father's many sins. He cannot be healed unless his father performs the proper penance.

I asked her: What is the proper penance?

But she made no further reply.

I will not shame you by making this matter known to anyone else, but I beg you, as the boy's father, to search your soul and find the unforgiven sin that stains it somehow. Only then can your son be saved.

The words of the *baal shem* left me with a heavy heart. I immediately went to the synagogue and, weeping and trembling, prayed with all my strength for the Holy One, Blessed be He, to have mercy upon my son and reveal to me what my grave sin was and how it could be repaired.

And then I felt a great weariness suddenly overcome me. I sat down on a bench in the back corner of the synagogue, put down my *siddur*, and fell into a deep sleep.

In my dream, I found myself standing again in the same grassy meadow. But when I turned to walk towards the noble lady's manor house, it was not there. Instead, I was now standing in the middle of a circle of tall trees. It appeared to be dusk, as the sky had turned pink. I stared up at the setting sun, and when I looked down again, there she was, the mysterious noblewoman, standing in front of me. But this time she appeared calm, her dress was clean and pressed, and her long black hair was neatly pinned in a big ball at the back of her head.

I asked what had happened to her house.

She replied that, in my sinful state, it was no longer permitted to me to cross its threshold.

I asked her: Why have you brought me here? I must awaken and return to my prayers to help my son.

She smirked and then she said: I have been sent to you in answer to your prayer. If you wish to save your son, then you must atone for the sin of revealing yourself as a saint and letting your pride and vanity swell. And this shall be your penance: In the next town over, in the *shtetl* of L, there is a brothel. You must go there and ask to see Maria. Pay whatever sum is necessary for you to be taken to Maria. Once you are in her room, you will lie with Maria. Do this, and your son's health and vigor will be restored. Fail to do this, and your son will die.

And then I woke up.

I thought this dream was crazy—I had to atone for giving too much public charity by committing the sin of adultery with a *shikse* whore? How could this be? This couldn't be. No messenger from the Heavenly Tribunal would ever say such a thing. She could only be a demon whose words were poison.

And so, I ignored my dream and did instead what I had always understood to be proper acts of repentance: I fasted, I recited Psalms, I gave away even more money to charity.

But nothing helped. My son only grew sicker and weaker.

Until one day, his eyes closed and he fell into a deep sleep. He barely breathed—and when he did, he made such wretched wheezing sounds that his little body rattled beneath his blanket. My wife gently poured chicken broth down his throat to keep him from starving, but otherwise we could do nothing.

Once more we summoned all the learned physicians. They told us the case was hopeless and the best we could hope for was that the boy would not suffer too much torment.

I was sure his suffering was on account of my many sins. Yet nothing I had done to repent had helped—my son's illness had only grown worse. Desperate to save my son, I finally decided to try what the noblewoman from my dream had suggested: I would go to the brothel and lie with this Maria.

Still, I hesitated: While most commandments of the Torah can be broken in order to save a life, the prohibition against adultery is not among them. But when I looked into my wife's eyes, and I saw her sorrow and pain, how could I not try? What father can just let his child die if there might be some way to save him?

I imagined the burial society picking my dead son up from the floor, wrapped in a shroud, and shoving him inside a tiny, child-sized coffin. At this vision, I fell to the ground writhing in pain, sobbing hysterically.

When my nerves had calmed, I reflected further: Perhaps this was a test of my faith. Abraham, may his merit protect us, had been ordered to sacrifice his son Isaac—an unspeakable sin, a horrible crime. But right before the knife was about to cut through Isaac's neck, an angel appeared and spared him. Maybe the same thing would happen with me? I would go, at the command of the Holy One, Blessed be He, to commit a terrible sin. Yet once I had proven my faith, at the very last moment a heavenly messenger would intervene to make sure I did not sin and my son would be saved just as Isaac was saved.

I resolved to go to the brothel and brave this test of my faith.

And so, I hired a peasant to take me in his wagon to the *shtetl* of L. Once I arrived, I went looking for the brothel. As I could not ask for directions to such a place—my shame would have been too great—I wandered around for a long time until I came upon a large house on the outskirts of the town. There, I beheld women flaunting themselves wantonly in the upstairs windows, with their faces heavily painted and their dresses immodest. They beckoned to me to come to them.

Putting my faith in the Holy One, Blessed be He, to see me through this ordeal, I forced myself to walk up the steps of the porch of that vile place and knock on the door. As I stood there waiting, I saw two Jews in their gabardines walk past. When they noticed me, a fellow Jew, loitering at the threshold of this house of sin, they averted their gaze and hung their heads in shame.

At that moment, I almost ran away. But then I remembered my son, suffering so horribly, and I held my ground, and I waited.

After a while, an old, fat blonde woman opened the door and invited me in. She spoke some kind of a greeting in her broken Yiddish and ushered me into a parlor room. There, she pushed me down into an upholstered red chair that stank of a harlot's perfume and handed me a glass of vodka. I mumbled a blessing—even though I felt ashamed to speak the holy tongue in a place of such filth—and quickly drank down the liquor, which helped steady me and clear my thoughts.

Meanwhile, the plump woman had walked over to the bottom of a staircase and was screaming up the stairs in Polish. When she was finished, five or six pretty young women came down and stood before me, flaunting themselves in their immodest garments.

The plump woman spoke to me in Yiddish again and asked which one I wanted.

I replied that I wanted Maria.

She shook her head and told me I did not want Maria. She said I should pick one of these others instead.

But I insisted. It had to be Maria.

After we repeated this back and forth a couple of more times, she finally gave up and dismissed the others, who left with a shrug—while I trembled with terror at the thought of what I was about to do, they seemed to be merely bored by all their sinning. The plump woman then disappeared down a dark hallway, loudly cursing all the stupid, stubborn, Christ-killing *Zhyds*.

A couple of minutes later, she returned with another woman in tow. This other woman was also fat and her face was pockmarked. And although her head was covered by a dirty kerchief, I could tell that underneath it she had precious little hair.

The blonde woman who seemed to be in charge said to me: This is Maria. You want her, you go with her.

And then she stormed off.

Maria grabbed my hand, pulled me up from the chair, and dragged me into the dark corridor from which she had emerged until we reached a door at the end, which she pushed open. Inside this room, there was a mattress on the floor and a small table. There were no windows and the only light came from a single dim candle.

After Maria closed the door behind us, she pulled off her dress and underwear, and stood before me in all her nakedness.

I did not know what to do. I was hoping for an angel to appear to put a stop to this sin, but none came. I stood there trembling in my fear and confusion as Maria looked at me with growing boredom and impatience. Eventually, she grabbed me again and threw me down onto the mattress.

Looking up at this huge naked *shikse*, with her immense folds of wrinkled fatty flesh, I was filled with disgust at myself—how could I have thought that adultery could save my son? I had to leave. I tried to get up, but Maria sat on top of me and pinned me down. She pulled off my pants and began to knead my flesh with her big sweaty hands.

But then a great miracle occurred: My flesh refused to respond and resisted sinning. After she had tired herself out with her futile efforts, she stood back up again and screamed at me in Polish, cursing my lack of manliness.

Seizing the opportunity to escape, I jumped up from the mattress, grabbed my pants from the floor, ran out of the room, back down the hallway, and out the front door of the house.

Maria, still naked, ran after me, hurling insults at the top of her lungs.

Soon a large crowd gathered to watch me being chased and abused. They laughed at the two of us and urged Maria to drag me back to the whorehouse for a sound whipping. They shouted: Faster, Maria, faster! Catch the little Jew! Don't let him get away!

Somehow I escaped from them all and found my way to a dense forest grove where I could stop, rest, and put my pants back on. I fell to my knees and sobbed and begged the Holy One, Blessed be He, to forgive me and show me mercy—for I had only been trying to save my son.

I walked back to my home, and did not cross my own threshold again until long after night had fallen. But when I entered, much to my shock, my wife and her parents were raising cups of wine in celebration. It is a miracle, they said to me, the boy suddenly woke up, completely healthy and cured, as if he had never been ill. The doctors returned and examined him and found nothing wrong. They swore they had never seen a case like this before, where a child so sick—so close to death—instantly recovers perfect health.

I fell to the ground and burst into joyful tears. Had I worked this miracle for my family? Was it because I had obeyed the woman in my dream? Or was it because my flesh, when put to the test, had refused to commit the sin of adultery?

Still, my happiness was brief. I had been recognized in the other *shtetl*, and word soon reached my town that I had been seen running half naked out of a brothel, chased by a naked *shikse* prostitute, at the same time that my wife had been fervently praying for our tiny son's recovery. Now I was no longer hailed as a *tzaddik*, a righteous saint, but cursed everywhere I went as the vilest of hypocrites, a filthy lecher who had pretended to be a man of great piety.

My wife and my in-laws were outraged and disgusted. I considered trying to explain to them how I had received a command in my dream to save our son by going to that brothel, but I decided that they would think I had gone mad. And so, I resigned myself to my fate. I was forced to sign a *get* granting my wife a divorce and returning her dowry in full, and then I was packed into a wagon and sent back to my father's house. My now former father-in-law also told me that I was never to write or speak to his daughter again and that the children would be told that I had been murdered by robbers along a forest road somewhere.

As you can imagine, my father was not pleased to see me. He rebuked me sternly for the shame I had brought down upon his head. What do you expect to do now? He asked me. Do you think any respectable family will ever marry their daughter to you? You will be lucky to marry a toothless beggar woman who stinks like a goat! And what decent Jew will do any business with you? Oy, I curse the day you were born.

But nevertheless, I did not feel any despair. So, what did I feel then? I felt that a heavy burden had been lifted from my heart: If I had lost my portion in both this world and the World to Come, and there was nothing I could do about it, then why should I worry about anything? What would be the point? There was nothing to do but wait until my allotted days had run their course.

And so, I slept late into the mornings. I took long walks by myself in the nearby woods and tried to make friends with the birds and the squirrels. Days slipped into weeks and weeks into months. I cannot remember for how long I drifted in this idle life. But soon enough, everything would change.

VI. A New Life

WHAT HAPPENED WAS this: My father had a brother who lived far away from us. This uncle of mine had grown wealthy leasing distilleries and taverns from the local nobleman. He had married a beautiful bride, much younger than him, and they had several young children.

But then he suddenly died. No one could understand it—one day he was healthy, strong as an ox, but the next night he died in his sleep. His widow was left in terrible straits. Her husband owed enormous payments to the nobleman for the leasehold rights, but there was no one left to run the business—at least no one whom she could trust, as the other Jews there had always been scheming to wrest these lucrative leaseholds away from my late uncle. Now, they would surely swoop in like vultures to pick over his carcass and steal from his widow.

In her desperation, she wrote to my father. Was there any male relative who could come to her aid to help run the business?

My father saw his opportunity. I was a burden to him, eating his food but earning no money and having no prospects to marry again. Perhaps I could be of use to the widow—at least it would get me away from his house and relieve the shame he felt each time he was forced to look upon my face.

So, off I went to that remote corner of White Russia. When I arrived at her house in the *shtetl* of M, the young widow curtly told me that I would be sleeping in a cramped, stuffy room in the attic. But I did not complain. I was not sure if she knew about my past shame. On the one hand, she said nothing about it. But on the other hand, she was not the least bit friendly, even though I was the relative who had traveled all the way there to help her. So maybe she did know? Well—it does not matter now.

I immediately got to work in my late uncle's business. After all, what else was I going to do? I had no wife and children there. And I did not wish to study any longer—the words of the holy sages of blessed memory, their admonitions, their teachings, struck me too painfully as a reproach for my many sins.

I quickly found some discrepancies in the ledgers, which led me to discover that one of the distillery workers was skimming liquor from our barrels and selling it on the side far below our prices. After firing this *gonif*, I wrote to the local nobleman to protest that the leasehold's promised monopoly on liquor sales in His Lordship's estate had been breached and that the widow had been wronged. The *Pan* agreed that we had been cheated out of our lawful profits and he accordingly remitted and delayed, somewhat, the leasehold payment that was otherwise due and owing.

The widow was overjoyed. While she carried herself with the modesty fitting for a Jewish mother, she started to show me little signs of her favor here and there. She would greet me with a warm smile when I came home. She cooked my favorite dishes. She even moved me downstairs to a more spacious room where the air was not quite so thick and hot.

In fact, as the widow's business continued to prosper under my guidance, she grew even bolder with her affections. At night, when I was exhausted from a long day of toil, she would serve me warm spiced mead and sit near me on the couch, close by but still careful not to be touching. She said I ran the business even better than her husband of blessed memory. She sometimes even praised my handsome appearance.

She encouraged her children—there were three of them, two boys and a girl—to speak with me and heed my words. The younger boy had just started *cheder*. I helped him to learn the Hebrew alphabet. I would tell him—and his brother and sister too—about the great heroes of Israel, about King David and Samson and Moses and the Prophet Elijah.

Eventually, the widow suggested that the two of us should marry. How could I say no? After my shameful past, I thought I would never have the chance to make a good match again. And this match was better than good—the widow was both beautiful and rich.

I wrote to my father to let him know the happy news. He wrote back congratulating me, but then added that we should hurry up and get married at once—don't wait for a date when he could attend the wedding, because he was no longer vigorous enough for such a long journey; and my mother had not been well; and there was probably another reason or two, which I have long since forgotten, for why he could not attend the wedding. I am sure he was worried the widow would hear about my past and call off the engagement, and so he wanted to rush things as much as possible.

As the widow also did not have any family nearby, we married without any further delay. Some of the town's Jews grumbled under their breadth about the strangeness of a wedding without relatives, but most of them seemed pleased that she had remarried and that there would be a father to raise her children.

Yet once again I was playing the part of a deluded fool who failed to understand what I needed to do. But I was fated to be brought back to my true path of righteousness.

VII. When Dreams Come True

ONE DAY I was summoned to the manor house of the local nobleman, as His Lordship and his steward wished to investigate the profitability of the distilleries and taverns on the estate. I was shown into the study, and the three of us sat around a fine wooden desk for the next several hours reviewing ledgers of sales and expenses and discussing whether there were perhaps other ways to make even more profit. The *Pan* seemed unusually obsessed that day with money—where was it hiding, where could it be found, from whom could it be squeezed. And whatever I suggested was never enough—always he had to have more, so much more.

Eventually, the *Pan* grew weary of this discussion and retired for a nap, leaving me alone with the steward of the estate. This steward was a good man—he was also a nobleman by birth, but he had fallen on hard times, and so now he was managing his cousin's lands. I asked the steward: Why was His Lordship suddenly so worried about the profits from his estate? Wasn't I already paying him a hefty fee for the leasehold rights that I held?

The steward sighed, leaned in close to me, and then said in a hushed voice, almost a whisper: After living alone as a widower for many years, the *Pan* has married again. But his bride . . . She was not born from any of the great noble families of Poland that had been seeking a marriage alliance with His Lordship. He had been resident in Warsaw, attending to his interests at the royal court, when a mysterious woman began to sit every day in the same café that he often frequented. She was beautiful and clearly high born—her every gesture was elegance itself and her French was impeccable—but no one knew her family or from whence she hailed. There were rumors that she was a Portuguese countess driven into exile after being betrayed to the Inquisition. But then others swore they had seen her dance at balls in Budapest or Moscow.

Whoever she was, the *Pan* fell madly in love with her. He would spend all day sitting in that café, waiting, hoping, to see her from afar. And when she did come, always alone, always with a book in hand, he stared at her with such pitiful longing that he made a humiliating spectacle of himself—like a stupid boy infatuated with the first pretty girl he had ever seen.

Every once in a while, she would stare back at him and smile coquettishly. She seemed to do just enough to keep his hopes alive, but went no further—at least in the beginning.

The *Pan* ordered his valet to find out who she was and where she lived. But no one in Warsaw knew her or could say anything reliable about her past or her affairs. The valet tried several times to follow her from the café back to her lodgings, but he became lost every time—somehow, she always slipped unseen around a corner or through an alleyway.

Finally, one afternoon, the *Pan* fortified himself with a strong brandy and approached her table. She invited him to sit down. He spoke to her of his great love, although he was awkward and nervous. But she interrupted him and said that if he was truly so besotted with her, then he ought to do the decent thing and propose marriage. He stared back at her in silence—I imagine he could not think of what to reply to such a bold and unexpected suggestion. Then she stood up, grabbed him by the hand, and said that it was agreed—they must get married that very instant.

She dragged him out of the café and into the nearest church where a priest was at the ready and they wed that day. After the ceremony, she sent him back to his Warsaw residence, where she joined him a few hours later with a large trunk in hand, containing, so she said, all her earthly belongings.

The next day, she said that she had grown tired of Warsaw and wished to pass some time in the country, amidst the forests and the fields. Could they not visit his country estate?

So, the *Pan* packed up his Warsaw residence and returned here. But throughout the journey, his new wife badgered him about fine dresses and jewels and art and furniture, not just from Warsaw but from Paris and Vienna and London—only the finest pieces could satisfy her refined taste. When he pleaded that he was not wealthy enough to satisfy all of her desires, she hissed back at him that he must endeavor to find ways to earn more income from his estates. And that is why, when he arrived, he immediately summoned you. Hopefully, this lovesick madness will soon fade away. I am sure that appropriate grounds can be found to annul this hasty and ill-advised marriage.

The steward then signaled to me that he could say no more and led me out of the study and back outside through the front door. When we reached the porch, he ordered a servant to hitch a horse to a wagon to take me home. As we waited for this servant to return from the stables, the steward poked me in the ribs and whispered: There she is.

I looked over and saw a woman approaching us, her tall body draped in the blood red of the setting sun. She wore an immodest dress, although not anything different than what other noble ladies would wear. Her thick dark hair fell to her waist.

But as she came closer, I was seized with such a great terror that I nearly fell to the ground. For I had seen this new wife of the *Pan* before: She was the woman from my dreams—the noble lady from the manor house in the meadow, the one who had insisted that

I was a hidden saint, a *lamed-vovnik*. But how had a figment of my imagination married His Lordship?

Or worse—maybe she was, as I had suspected, a demon, and now she had seduced the *Pan*. The Jews living on his lands could be in grave danger—who knew what persecutions she was planning for our holy community?

Yet when she noticed me staring at her, she did not greet me or give any other sign that she knew me. Instead, speaking in Polish with a strange foreign accent, she shouted at me that filthy *Zhyds*, shameless killers of Christ, should learn to lower their eyes and treat highborn ladies with proper respect.

And then she stormed off inside the house.

In the next instant, the wagon came from the stables, much to my relief, and led me away.

Even though the woman from my old dreams had reappeared before my eyes in flesh and blood, I did not dream of her that night, nor any of the next several nights. I tried to dream about her. I forced myself to recall my earlier dreams in as much detail as possible. I even prayed to the Holy One, Blessed be He, to send me dreams of her, but all to no avail. It was as if she had departed from my mind in order to mount the *Pan*'s marital bed.

It was another three weeks before I saw her again. This time, I was in one of the taverns I leased from His Lordship, trying to make sure that the fat, lazy fool who managed it—some relative of a friend of my wife—was still performing his duties well enough.

After a couple of hours of reviewing accounts and inventories, I was tired and sat down to drink some mead. But then the door swung open and in she walked, His Lordship's new wife, the strange lady from my dreams. She was accompanied by a big bear of a peasant, one of the *Pan*'s coachmen. The tavern keeper served them wine, bread, and cheese.

They were the only customers at that hour and they ate in silence. To stop myself from again staring at Her Ladyship, I gazed hard instead at the stains and smudges on the wall opposite me. Still, my heart raced frantically.

And then the *Pani* and her coachman abruptly stood up and left. But just as I was about to refill my cup to celebrate that no new shame or abuse had come down upon my head, the carriage driver walked back in, pointed at me, and said that the Lady demanded that I come outside to speak with her.

Having no other choice—for how could I refuse to speak to the *Pan*'s wife? —I left the inn and followed him to a coach waiting outside. The big coachman pulled me up by my shoulders and shoved me inside the back next to his mistress.

The next thing I knew the carriage was off.

I was terrified. Where was I being taken? And for what purpose? Still, with an effort, I steadied my nerves. I thought: She was going to do whatever she was going to do, and all I could do was trust that the Holy One, Blessed be He, in His Infinite Mercy, would keep me safe from harm.

The carriage drove out of the town and onto the forest road. We soon came to a wide meadow, like the one in my dreams, except without a manor house. Here we stopped but stayed inside the coach.

So far, she had not spoken to me and I had not spoken to her. But now she said to me in her strange foreign-accented Polish: You are the Jew who leases the distilleries and taverns from my husband. You keep the serfs drunk and stupid, and you keep my husband rich. I know your kind—you scrape the floor with your chin, you flatter and cajole and scheme. You are a clever man—the kind of man who knows better than to gape at his lord's wife like a lovestruck boy. Tell me then, why did you stare at me that way?

I looked down at my knees and stammered out an apology and begged her pardon for my rude behavior and swore it would never happen again.

She let out a sigh, but one that sounded kind, even motherly. She said to me: I don't want your apology. I want to know why you did what you did. When you look at my face, what do you see? Who do you see? Tell me.

Then she grabbed my chin and forced me to look straight into her burning black eyes.

My body trembled and shook.

Well? She said. Speak, tell me.

I told her I was too embarrassed to say.

She smacked me across the face and told me that I would be whipped and beaten if I did not do as I was told.

And so, with a heavy heart, I confessed that I had seen her in my dreams, in a beautiful house in a wide meadow. I hastened to add that nothing shameful had ever happened in these dreams but rather she had scolded me for my many sins and urged me to repent.

She laughed. You dreamed that I was a nun, she said, punishing you for your wickedness. Although it sounds as if I had run away from my convent. You are a mad fool.

And then she ordered the driver to take me back to my home. We did not speak again during that carriage ride.

A few days later, I saw the *Pan*'s steward in one of my taverns. He told me that the *Pan* and his new wife had departed the countryside to return to their Warsaw residence. He did not know when they planned to return, although he added that he would not miss what he called that miserable woman. He had been exhausted by her never-ending demands—that the cook prepare different dishes, that the rooms be redecorated, that expensive paintings and linens and furniture be purchased from Warsaw and Moscow and Vienna, and so on and so forth.

I resolved to think no more about the new *Pani* and whatever she might be doing in faraway Warsaw. But then one night, after I had drifted into a deep sleep, I dreamed that I was standing again in a meadow of tall, gently rustling grass. It was sunny and warm there, and the sky was a clear blue. I saw the manor house in the distance, the same one from my previous dreams. I crossed over to it and walked through an open door to the parlor room inside.

This time the room was in perfect condition—not a scratch on the walls or a rip in the furniture. And there, sitting on the couch, I saw *her*. She was wearing a white robe, and her long black hair smelled of the most wonderful, luxurious perfume.

She motioned for me to sit down next to her.

After I was seated, I demanded to know why she had brought me back again to this place. I warned her that I was content with my portion in this life and did not intend to change how I was spending my allotted days.

She smiled at me and said, in a soft, cooing voice: But you must change your ways. You are one of the thirty-six hidden saints upon whose merit the world depends. And yet you continue to refuse to live the life of a hidden *tzaddik*. Thus, I have been sent once more to help you. I have even descended into your lowly material world and married your *Pan*. When you meet me again in your waking hours, you must do exactly what I tell you to do. Only then will you be returned to the path of righteousness.

But I protested in response: I am living a righteous life, following the Torah, raising children, looking after my wife. Your words have only ever led me to sin and misery and shame. And when I saw you at the *Pan*'s manor house, you did not even recognize me. Whatever you are, you are not His Lordship's flesh and blood wife—you are some cunning demon trying to muddle my reason.

She leaned back against the couch and looked at me carefully. But she did not appear to be upset. No, rather, she looked like a loving mother trying to figure out the right words to soothe a stubborn and stupid child.

Eventually, she said: For now, you have heard what you needed to hear. Trust that, in good time, you will be guided onto the righteous path. This is the decree of the Heavenly Court.

And then I woke up.

VIII. The Fall

A FEW MONTHS after my dream, the *Pan* and his wife returned to their country estate. Their arrival was like nothing I had ever beheld before—a long train of gilded carriages stretching back as far as the eye could see. The steward told me that she had dragged her husband across many famous cities—not just Warsaw and Krakow, but also Berlin and Vienna and Budapest—to purchase dresses, jewels, paintings, sculptures, wines, perfumes, porcelain dishes from China, and who knew what else.

The day after His Lordship returned, I was summoned back to the manor house to review my account books with him and his steward. The *Pan* was heartened to learn that his distilleries were producing far more barrels of vodka than he had thought and that his peasants were spending all their spare money in his taverns drinking it. I even pointed out that there were surplus barrels, which perhaps could be sold to brokers and factors for resale somewhere else, perhaps Konigsberg.

After we finished, I was brought to a parlor room to wait for a wagon to be readied to take me home. While I was sitting there, three servants approached me, huge *goyim*, each one as big and strong as an ox. They offered me a glass of wine. I politely declined, as their wine was not kosher. But they insisted—this wine is excellent, they said, a gift from the *Pan*—very rude to refuse such a generous gift.

I repeated that I could not drink it because it was not kosher.

Then one of the men grabbed me from behind and another squeezed my nose to force my mouth open, and poured the *treyf* drink down my throat.

Everything suddenly went dark, my limbs became heavy as lead, and I felt myself collapse upon the floor before I lost all consciousness.

When I awoke, I was lying in a bed in a windowless room, and my head pounded terribly. With difficulty, I sat up and yawned. Just then, the door to this room opened and in walked the *Pan*'s wife. She sat down next to me and handed me a glass of water. After I had drunk it down, I asked her where I was and why she had brought me to this place.

Instead of answering, she grabbed my head and kissed me. I knew this was a terrible sin, but her lips were so soft, and the way she stroked my flesh with her firm hands . . . suffice it to say, I gave into temptation.

When it was over, I felt such shame that I burst into tears and averted my gaze from her.

But she was not angry with me, nor did she leave. She put her arms around my back and cradled me like a newborn baby. Then she slipped a morsel of food into my mouth—before I could even say the proper blessing—but it was such wondrous food, a fresh, moist cheese that tasted like the sweetest honey. After swallowing several mouthfuls, I drifted back to sleep.

And then the same events came to pass again—I awoke, she lay with me, I was wracked with guilt and remorse, and she fed me the honey-flavored cheese until I fell asleep. I am not sure how many times this was repeated—my reason was clouded and the memories are a blur.

Eventually, I woke up in a new place: my own bed in my own house. This time, I was greeted by my wife. I felt so ashamed that I could not bear to meet her gaze. But she smiled at me and said she was glad that I was feeling better.

I asked her how I had come to be back in our home.

She said the *Pan*'s servants had brought me, after I had fallen ill at the manor house.

I asked her: Had I been brought here directly from the manor house? Or had I been taken somewhere else first?

But my wife said: Why would you have been taken elsewhere? You visited the *Pan* in his manor house, you fell ill, and then he had you brought back here.

She added that she was going out to the marketplace to buy some food and urged me to go downstairs to eat something.

After she left, I thought: I must have dreamed I was taken to that windowless room. The *Pan*'s wife had appeared in my dreams many times before and she must have done so again. I had not actually sinned against my wife—it was only a dream. A dream conjured up by my *yetzer hara*, my evil inclination, yes, but dreaming about a sin is not the same as doing the sin. It had to be a dream. Why would the beautiful wife of a wealthy lord want to sin with me? I was not handsome. And compared to her husband, I was a pauper. The only sensible explanation was that I had fallen ill and dreamed more wild bizarre dreams in my delirium.

And so, having reassured myself that I had in fact committed no transgression, I got up, dressed, went downstairs, and ate some bread and jam. With a bit of food in my belly, I felt strong enough to go back to tending to my business, praying in the synagogue, and all the rest of my daily routine.

Weeks passed. I tried not to think about the *Pan* and his wife, and I hoped they would depart again soon for some great city far away from my *shtetl*. But instead, they lingered in the countryside.

After a while, I was summoned back to the manor house. Yet when I arrived, the *Pan* was away hunting with his steward, and I was told they were not expected back for many hours. I asked the servants why I had been summoned if His Lordship was not there? But they just told me to sit and wait.

I sat there for a long time, bored and nervous. Eventually, a servant came and led me to a bedroom in the far back of that huge house, a place in which I had never set foot before that day. The curtains in the room were drawn tightly over the windows and the only light was from a dim orange candle.

After the servant had left and closed the door behind him, a figure suddenly emerged from beneath the thick blankets on the bed—the *Pan*'s wife. I froze in terror. Why had she brought me here? Had I actually sinned with her before—and not just in my dreams? What if the servant betrayed us? Her husband would have me imprisoned or beaten or worse.

She grabbed my face and kissed me. And then she said: My husband will visit your tavern tomorrow. Here are spices—and she handed me a small jar—which you must mix into his drink. But do not let him see what you are doing. Now you must go.

And before I could ask any questions, she shoved me out of the room into the arms of the same servant waiting in the hallway, who led me back to the front of the house and into a wagon which drove me home.

During the ride home, and for the rest of that day and night, I pondered whether I should do what she had asked me to do. The jar was quite small, maybe the length of my index finger. Its contents looked like crushed flower petals, but they were a sickly yellowish green, like a diseased toe that needs to be cut off before its rot infects the rest of the body. I tried smelling it, but there was no scent.

Was she trying to poison him? But why ask me to do it? She lived with the *Pan* and could poison him anytime she liked. And why should she even want to poison him? He was madly in love with her, indulged her every whim, and was wealthy. What else could she want?

But if the spice jar was not full of poison, why conceal it from His Lordship?

I resolved to toss it away, down into some muddy ditch, and be done with this strange business. But still, I hesitated. If I did not do what she had asked, and she discovered my unfaithfulness, then she might seek vengeance against me. She would claim that I had snuck into her bedroom and tried to force myself upon her—and she would have that servant as a witness. I would be imprisoned, flogged, most likely killed. And what would happen to my wife and her children? Or to the other Jews in the town—for the *Pan* would surely unleash his wrath upon all of his Jews, perhaps even drive them away and seize their property.

I could not let such suffering come to pass. I had to obey her instructions.

Yet on the other hand, my thoughts continued, it is not permitted to commit murder even to save a life. So, how could I go ahead and poison His Lordship? But then again, how did I know I was going to murder him by adding these spices to his drink? No one had told me that this was poison. *She* had not said anything about wanting to harm her husband, much less kill him. She had asked me to spice his drink—where is the harm in that? Wine is spiced all the time.

Now I laughed at myself for being so foolish as to think that I was being made an accomplice to murder. This must be some clever lovers' game between the *Pan* and his wife. He would taste this particular spice in his drink and know that she had slipped it to me to serve to him and he would crack a knowing smile—because it was all a joke between them. I would do as the Lady of the manor house had commanded, and play my part in her flirtatious game.

The next day, after morning prayers, I went to one of my taverns to inspect its account books, with the little spice jar nestled in my coat pocket. Shortly after I had arrived and begun my work, in walked the *Pan* and several of his servants. They greeted me warmly and asked for some wine to slake their thirst.

I told the tavern keeper that I would take care of pouring the wine for our guests. And when I did so, I mixed the spices from the little jar into His Lordship's cup. The *Pan* quickly drank that cup of spiced wine to the dregs.

And then nothing happened. He did not die or double over in pain or vomit. He did not even comment that his wine tasted any differently than it usually did.

Feeling relieved that my worries over the tiny spice jar had turned out to be groundless, I spent the rest of the day sorting out the affairs of that tavern. Then I went to the synagogue for evening prayers and finally returned home. Once the children were asleep, I studied a page or two of *Chumash* with Rashi's commentary, until weariness overcame me and I went to bed.

The brief sleep I enjoyed that night held the last pleasurable hours I have known in this world. For in the middle of the night, I was awakened by a man violently shaking me. I jumped up—I thought it was a robber—but no, it was the *shammes* of the synagogue. I could just make out his face in the moonlight coming in through the window. He woke my wife as well, and led us downstairs to the kitchen.

Once we were all seated around the table, the *shammes* told me that, after the *Pan* had left my tavern that morning, he had ridden into the woods to go hunting. But after an hour or so of chasing deer, he suddenly felt quite sick and ordered the party to return to the manor house. That night, he burned with fever and suffered from terrible stomach pains. They sent for the doctor, but before the doctor could arrive, he had died.

His household was in an uproar—what could have happened? Had he eaten or drunk something that could have poisoned and killed him?

And then one of the servants said that the last food or drink His Lordship had touched was a cup of wine in my tavern, served from my own hands.

This led a second servant to speak up and say that he had seen me in the bedroom of the *Pan*'s wife—although he swore her honor was unstained and that I had been soundly rebuffed when I made my filthy advances. Her Ladyship blushed at these words, cried a little, and silently nodded her head in agreement.

The steward then said that it seemed to him that I had murdered my lord in a jealous rage. He urged the others to get some rest and promised I would be seized from my bed at the first light of dawn and brought to justice.

Fortunately for me, there was an old servant of the *Pan* whom the *shammes* secretly bribed to let him know if some trouble was brewing that could threaten the Jews of our *shtetl*. This man snuck away when the others went to bed and told the *shammes* about everything that had transpired that night, and then the *shammes* went to my house to warn me.

My wife said there was no time to waste—my only hope was to hitch a horse to our wagon and flee immediately, to try to get far enough away by dawn that they would not capture me. The *shammes* agreed.

In my confusion and despair, with my thoughts all in a jumble, I did what they told me to do, and before I fully understood what was happening, I found myself alone on a wagon, rushing through the forest highway by the light of the moon. All I had with me were a flask of wine, a couple of loaves of bread, and a few small rinds of hard cheese.

IX. A Hidden Saint's Days of Righteousness

I KEPT TO the forest road until the sun began to rise. At that point, I decided it was no longer safe to travel on the main highway, where I could be easily overtaken by the powerful horses from the *Pan*'s stables. So, I abandoned the horse and the wagon on the side of the road, gathered my provisions in my arms, and fled by foot deep into the woods.

For the next three days I wandered into the wilderness. Eventually, I sat down and rested in the middle of a dense cluster of trees. I had just finished the last of my food. I cursed the hour in which I had been born and asked the Holy One, Blessed be He, why He took such delight in tormenting me.

Exhaustion overcame me and I fell into a deep sleep. In my dream, I was standing once more in that same wide meadow with the tall grass. The air was warm, the sun was shining, and there were no clouds in the sky. In the distance, I saw the same manor house that I had beheld in my previous dreams, but it had never before shimmered so brightly, as if the walls had been freshly painted—no, as if they had been freshly gilded.

I walked over to the manor house, went up the steps of the porch, and entered through the front door into the parlor room. And there on the couch I saw her again, the double of the wife of the murdered *Pan*.

She smiled and asked me to sit down next to her.

But this time, I refused. Instead, I asked her why she had murdered her husband and then cunningly arranged matters so that I would be blamed. Because of her wickedness, I had been forced to flee from my wife and my fellow Jews, and I would soon starve to death alone in the forest. After this pitiful death, I would be cursed in the next world to suffer for my many and horrible sins—sins I had committed because of her.

Yet my harsh words did not seem to anger her. To the contrary, she leaned back into the cushions on the couch and gently sighed. And then she said: You grasp only the surface meaning and not the deeper truth. You are one of the thirty-six hidden saints, a *lamed-vovnik*, but for too long you strayed from your proper path. You were too proud and you flaunted your good deeds to flatter that pride—and thus your *mitzvot* were not pleasing to the Throne of Glory. But now you will live alone, in hiding, for you are condemned as a murderer. You will not starve. When you awake, you will be lying in a hut in a remote clearing. This hut will be your home for the rest of your days. Like your forefathers wandering in the desert, you will be fed with manna and provided with water, just enough to keep your body and soul stitched together.

And in your solitude, you will practice righteousness—but this time it will be true righteousness, exalted righteousness, and not the petty, puny *mitzvot* of ordinary Jews with their dash of charity here or observance of a commandment there. No, you will be a *baal teshuvah*, a master of repentance. As the holy sages of blessed memory taught in the Talmud: In the place where the penitent stands, the completely righteous cannot stand. In other words: The good deeds of one who has never been tempted are not as pleasing to the Holy One, Blessed be He, as the righteousness of one who has tasted sin, who has fallen far into the depths and then clawed his way back up through a genuine atonement.

I entered your world and married your *Pan* so that I could lead you into a sinfulness so terrible that you could not bear its weight—first adultery with my incarnated flesh and then the murder of my husband. The wealthy householder who was once so smugly content in his own goodness is now a vile, loathsome criminal, despised and abandoned by all who knew him. But the vastness of your sins will make for the vastness of your repentance. And the greatest repentance is the greatest righteousness. This is your task: To atone through the suffering that will be inflicted upon you, and to endure these ordeals without the consolation of wife or friend or child. And you will know when your penitence is complete because on that night you will be visited by a mighty sage, and you will tell your tale to him and to his disciple so that they may repeat it again to others in the proper time and place. When you finish your tale, the sun will rise and your soul will drift away from your body.

I was bewildered by her words—for how can it be righteous to sin simply in order to have something to repent? And why did the *Pan* have to be murdered? Granted, he was a bit of a drunkard and not always kind to his Jews, but still, he was a man and should have been permitted to enjoy his portion of days. Not to mention my wife and her children—why must they suffer by losing a husband and father? And if I were to live out my days alone in the forest, my wife would become an *agunah*, a woman unable to remarry because her husband's death can never be confirmed.

I wanted to ask all these questions and more, but before I could, my eyes burst open and I was wide awake. I found myself lying inside this hut. On my left side were a jug of fresh water and a small loaf of bread. And each day afterward, when I awoke, that jug was full of cool water and a freshly baked loaf of bread was by my side.

I have lived alone in this hut ever since. Before tonight, I had never received any visitors. I have spent my long, sad days reflecting upon my sins—all of them, not just the great ones I have recounted to you but also the myriad of tiny ones that tend to slip away from our minds. I have concentrated intensely upon the memory of each and every sin and wept and prayed and begged the Holy One, Blessed be He, for forgiveness.

And my afflictions were not only spiritual. Snakes and other vermin would creep upon me while I slept and gnaw at my flesh. There were boils and sores all over my skin, and I could smell the stink of my own body rotting. I often burned with fever, there were sharp pains in my stomach, my chest hurt when I breathed, and my throat was sore and dry. But I happily submitted to these torments as just recompense for my many sins. Let my punishment be now, in this material world of illusion, so that my portion in the World to Come, the realm of truth, will be all the more splendid and magnificent.

The days came and went, each one just like the other, and I did not try to keep track of them. But now my atonement has reached its end. You, Rabbi Israel ben Eliezer, holy Baal Shem Tov, are no doubt the mighty sage whom the noble lady had foretold would come to me in my last night in this lowly world. And just as she had said it would come to pass, I have told my tale to you. It is time for my soul to depart from my body.

We shall meet again someday in the World to Come. I shall build a great palace there and fill my table with such delicacies as your tongue has never tasted. And you, holy sage, pillar of your generation, light of our exile, when it will finally be your time to ascend to the World to Come to enjoy your portion of paradise, I will welcome you into my palace and perform the *mitzvah* of hospitality. We shall join hands and walk together through the footpaths in the Garden of Eden until we reach the Celestial

Academy, where we shall hear Our Master and Teacher Moses himself expound upon secrets of the Torah.

Yes, in the next world, our delights will be unending . . .

X. The Death of the Hidden Saint

AND THOSE WERE the last words that the hidden saint, the *lamed-vovnik*, ever spoke. By then, the sun was rising and the early morning light was coming in through the holes in the ceiling of the hut. The hidden saint closed his eyes and curled up his body. His breathing became so faint that the Baal Shem Tov put a feather under his nose to see if he was still alive. When there was no longer any breath to move the feather, we knew that he had passed on to the next world.

I asked the Baal Shem Tov if we should wrap his body in a shroud and arrange for a proper Jewish burial.

But he told me to be still and wait.

A few moments later, to my amazement, the hidden saint's body suddenly shriveled like a prune, as if someone had drained all the blood out of him in an instant. Then I heard the sounds of bones cracking and breaking, and he turned into a pile of dust.

I tried, at the least, to gather this dust for a decent burial, but the grains fled from my fingers into the ground, as if they were terrified of my touch.

The Baal Shem Tov then told me that it was time to depart. He led me back outside the hut, where Stepan the coachman had already hitched the horses to the wagon. Once we were settled in behind him, the Baal Shem Tov uttered a combination of holy names, the coachman instantly let go of the reins and fell asleep, and the horses took off into the air.

The Baal Shem Tov did not speak again during the journey home. I had so many questions for my master and teacher—for the man we had met was not at all what I had thought a *lamed-vovnik* would be. He was a murderer and an adulterer and probably insane. And what *mitzvot* could he have performed sitting alone in that hut with his sores and boils and snakes and rats?

But I held my tongue, as I trusted that the Baal Shem Tov would reveal the hidden truth of these marvels when the proper time came. I was often baffled by the actions of my master, as he was able to penetrate into truths concealed far beneath the surface illusions of this sinful world. Once, I remember, he had advised that a sick child should receive a blessing from a notorious drunkard. The boy's father was outraged, but, as the *tzaddik* insisted, he visited the man at dawn—for by the middle of the morning he was already passed out from his drunkenness—and received his blessing. And as soon as the blessing was spoken, the child was cured. I asked my master and teacher of blessed memory: How could this be—how could a drunken boor's blessing have such power? And the Baal Shem Tov told me: The man who appears to you to be a drunken boor is in fact a great and mighty sage, one of the finest Torah scholars who has ever lived. But as he sometimes neglected his morning prayers in a prior incarnation, his soul was sent back down into this world in a new body to repair this sin by praying dutifully each morning. And once this task is done, he passes out drunk for the rest of the day. Since this man is such a revered sage, his blessing carries the power to undo the harsh punishments decreed by the Heavenly Tribunal.

And so, what often appeared bizarre and inexplicable to my foolish eyes was in truth something wondrous and holy. Indeed, the Baal Shem Tov taught that the Holy One, Blessed be He, is present in all things—*For there is no place without Him.* Thus, whatever appears on the surface to be sinful or perhaps just baffling and mysterious, in fact contains a spark of sublime and pure holiness.

Yet even after we returned to Mezhbizh, the Baal Shem Tov still did not explain the meaning of the hidden saint's crazy tale. Days passed, weeks passed, other urgent matters pressed upon us—for there was never any shortage of Jews in need of aid and protection—but the Baal Shem Tov said not a word about our long night with the dying *lamed-vovnik*.

Yet my troubled soul would not let the matter rest. I could not understand how such a vile criminal and sinner could be one of the thirty-six hidden righteous men upon whose merit the continued existence of the world depends. If this were one of the thirty-six, then I could not fathom why the Holy One, Blessed be He, had not already brought forth another flood to destroy the world, just as He had done in the days of Noah of blessed memory. But the world had not been destroyed. So, there must have been some great concealed truth in this matter that my feeble mind had failed to grasp. But what was it?

Eventually, my patience failed me—I had to know the meaning of this mystery. One evening, after prayers, I asked the Baal Shem Tov if I could speak with him privately about a matter that was weighing heavily upon my heart.

The Baal Shem Tov agreed at once and brought me into the study in the back of his house. He closed the door, drew the thick curtains, and placed a candle on the table between us. Reb Jacob, he said, what is troubling you?

And I said to my master and teacher of blessed memory: Rabbi Israel, holy Baal Shem Tov, I am troubled by the evening that we spent in the hut of the *lamed-vovnik*. I do not understand how a man who committed such terrible sins as murder and adultery could be one of the thirty-six upon whose righteousness the world rests. Please, take pity upon me and reveal the truth of this matter.

The Baal Shem Tov sighed loudly and looked down at his feet. He was silent for a long time. When he lifted his head back up again, this is what he said: I had received a message in a dream that on such and such a day I was to travel to a remote clearing in a forest to visit a sickly old Jew who lived alone there in a miserable hut. I was told he was about to die, but that before he did, it was necessary for me to hear him tell his tale. Who is this man? I asked. But the messenger—who hid his countenance from me—would reveal no more.

When I awoke the next morning, I reflected upon this strange dream. I wondered if this sickly Jew could be one of the thirty-six hidden righteous, a *lamed-vovnik*. After all, he was a Jew living in horrible suffering and poverty but somehow still so great in his deeds and piety that the Heavenly Court had sent its messenger to command me to attend to him in his last hours. What else could he be but a *lamed-vovnik*?

Like you, Reb Jacob, I could not understand how a saint had committed such grave sins as murder and adultery. *And* he did not study Torah, he did not aid other Jews, and he did not even seem to pray. He just sat in his hut, year after year, endlessly bewailing his sins. But an exaggerated atonement can itself be a sign of sinful pride.

After we returned from that hut, I locked myself in this room and prayed with such intense *kavannah* that my soul was able to ascend to the Heavenly Court. When I beheld the angels and the holy sages and the prophets strolling in the garden paths between the palaces of Paradise, I demanded that they reveal to me who that man in the wretched hut truly was and why I had been commanded to attend to him during his last night.

But they did not answer me. They hung their heads in shame and walked away.

I invoked the combination of holy names to summon and bind the angel Metatron. Once he was in my power, I demanded that he answer my questions. But he only sighed and said: The summons you received did not issue from the Throne of Glory, but from some other realm, from somewhere deep within the *sitra achra*, the other side. No more can I say.

I released Metatron and returned to this lowly world. I do not know how or why the forces of the other side deceived me, but thankfully that loathsome madman is dead—may the worms feast on the dust of his bones.

The Baal Shem Tov never again spoke of that diseased man in his hut who thought he was a *lamed-vovnik*.

XI. The Nobleman's Tale

AND WITH THOSE words, Reb Jacob finished his tale of the hidden saint and the holy Baal Shem Tov of blessed memory.

For the briefest of moments, everyone in the tavern was silent and still. And then there was an eruption of rage and abuse from the Jews gathered around Reb Jacob: You promised us a tale of the *tzaddik* Rabbi Israel ben Eliezer, the holy Baal Shem Tov, and one of the thirty-six hidden saints upon whose merit the world rests—a tale that would uplift our souls, a tale that would teach us the path of righteousness. But instead, you babbled on about some lice-ridden lunatic in the forest who committed murder and adultery and who knows what other sins! And this madman considered himself to be one of the thirty-six righteous? Why did you tell us something so awful? Even if everything happened just as you told it, you should not shame your master and teacher of blessed memory by spreading this tale, which only dishonors him.

Reb Jacob hung his head down and replied: I have never told this tale before—I had forgotten it until tonight. But when His Lordship asked me to tell a tale of one of the thirty-six hidden saints, my memory of the night with the diseased madman in the hut instantly returned, with every detail intact, and I felt some great power compel me to tell this tale. You are right to rebuke me: I have shamed the memory of the Baal Shem Tov. Before I go to sleep tonight, I shall pray to my master and teacher in the next world to forgive me.

The Polish nobleman who had originally asked for the tale to be told now stood up and spoke again: Reb Jacob, there is no reason to hang your head in shame. Just as I promised, I shall pay you handsomely for this tale of the Baal Shem Tov and the hidden saint. In fact, you have told me the precise tale that I was hoping to hear.

I see from your face, Reb Jacob, that you do not follow my meaning. After all, you had never recounted this tale before tonight. So, you must be wondering: How could this *Pan*, who is not even a Jew, possibly know of this particular tale of the Baal Shem Tov, which even you, his faithful disciple, had forgotten?

I shall tell you *my* tale now, which perhaps will make these matters clearer to you. And when I am done, I will stuff your purse full of gold coins.

I never knew my father, as he had died when my mother was pregnant with me. He was a wealthy nobleman who had been murdered—poisoned—by one of his Jewish leaseholders. The motive for the crime, according to what I was told, was that this Jew had fallen in love with my mother and killed his lord out of jealousy. However, the murderer escaped before he could be held to account and was never heard from again.

My mother never remarried. She was a foreigner, but no one knew the country of her birth or whether her family was of noble blood. When I would inquire as to the truth of her origins, she would only say: I am a stranger in a strange land, an eternal wanderer. One day I shall leave here too.

She hired private tutors and governesses to educate me. Like her, they were all foreigners. But unlike other noble families, my tutors were not German and my governesses were not French. Some of our neighbors speculated that they were Greeks, or Spaniards, or maybe even Turks. But they were as coy as my mother and would only say, like her, that they were strangers in a strange land.

Still, my mother and my tutors and my governesses were all remarkably learned. They spoke an extraordinary number of languages—Latin, Greek, Hebrew, Arabic, Turkish, Polish, Russian, French, German, English, Italian, Spanish, Portuguese, and even some Chinese. When His Holiness the Bishop would visit, they would astound him with the subtlety of their theological conjectures and their vast readings in the works of the Church fathers. Should an enlightened man of science happen to cross our threshold, he would be cowed into submission by their mastery of mathematics and astronomy. We once even hosted a composer, a man who had been feted and admired by the best society in Vienna, who was astonished by my mother's deep knowledge of music.

Yet despite all the genius gathered in our household, we largely avoided mixing with society. While we would receive guests from time to time, we never visited others. And the visits we did receive were in no way solicited by my mother. Rather, either someone wished for my mother to contribute her ample funds to some worthy enterprise—this was why the Bishop called upon us—or they were travelers passing through the region, men of a certain rank seeking hospitality in the remote countryside.

I grew up a sad and lonely boy. When I was not occupied with my studies, I took long, solitary walks around the grounds of our manor house. I tried to kill birds by throwing rocks at them, but I always failed. I once attempted to tend a little vegetable garden, but I could make nothing grow.

With so few diversions to pass the time, I took to studying the habits of my mother and her companions. The first peculiar thing I noticed was how they behaved in church. Like all good noble Polish Catholic families, we heard Mass each Sunday morning. Yet while the other Christians prayed with fervor and sometimes burst into tears before the stained-glass pictures of the Holy Virgin Mother, my mother and her friends looked bored. They spent their time in the pews whispering and snickering.

One night, I retired early to bed. My governess kissed my forehead, blew out the candle in my room, and left me alone. After I was sure that she had gone and I could no longer hear her footsteps trailing in the hallway, I snuck out to learn what my mother and her companions did at night after I was asleep.

Yet wherever I roamed, the house was empty. The hallways, parlor, library, dining room, study, even my mother's bedroom—all empty and silent. I was terrified—what had happened to my mother? Where had everyone gone? Had they abandoned me? Had a gang of robbers slit their throats?

I lit a small candle and ventured outside, terrified that at any moment some bandit was going to emerge from the shadows to sink a knife into my chest. But the nearby grounds—our gardens and stables and outhouses—were just as deserted as the inside of the manor house.

I walked on slowly, gingerly, breathing hard at every step. I kept hoping that my mother would suddenly appear, laugh at my fears, and march me right back to bed.

But there was no one there.

After what felt like an interminable stretch of time stumbling about in the dark, I at last heard sounds—voices—in the distance. I stopped and listened closely. It was my mother and my tutors and governesses.

I walked quickly toward the voices, until I reached the edge of the meadow in the back of our manor house, right where the old woods began. There, I saw my mother and the others emerging from a narrow footpath in the forest. Between the candle in my hand and the moon overhead, I could just make out that the tree by the entrance to this path had been marked with bizarre symbols that I did not recognize.

I decided to go back to my room before they saw me.

The next day, when I took my usual solitary walk, I returned to that same spot at the edge of the meadow. I found a tall beech tree there on which someone had painted various markings in red, like letters from a mysterious alphabet. Next to this tree, I saw the footpath again and followed it into the woods until I came upon a hill. Carved into the side of this hill was a wide artificial grey stone grotto decorated with the same strange red letters that I had seen on the tree. I noticed, in the far-left corner of the grotto, the faint outlines of a door. With a great effort by my small childish body, I was able to force it open.

Behind this door was a staircase illuminated by a dull orange light. I went down these stairs, which twisted and turned far beneath the ground. The passageway was cold and damp, and sometimes I felt rats scurrying about my feet. But I was determined to discover my mother's secret and so I forced myself forward.

When I reached the bottom, I found myself standing in a circular room chiseled out of the rock. On one side was a large cistern filled with water. Facing the cistern on the opposite wall was an immense stove, burning and hissing and giving off the orange light by which I was able to see my surroundings. Next to the stove were tidily stacked crates and barrels, but without any markings or signs to indicate what their contents might be.

I was baffled. Why go to the trouble—and no doubt significant expense—of creating this secret underground cavern just to hold a few crates and a stove and a big tub of water? If my mother wanted to wash herself, she had a far more elegant bath in our house.

But then I suddenly heard moaning sounds coming from the inside of the cistern. Out of curiosity, I went over to have a closer look. And that is when I learned that my mother had good reason for keeping this place hidden so far beneath the ground: For in the water, I saw a man writhing in a miserable hut somewhere. He appeared to be an old bearded Jew afflicted with some terrible disease. His skin was covered in boils and sores and he was screaming out in pain.

I bent over to get a closer look, wondering who he could be and how his reflection had appeared in the water. And then I saw his eyes turn in my direction. He pointed his finger at me and called out in Yiddish: Boy, who are you? How did you get here?

I jumped back in terror and ran as fast as I could back up the cold, damp staircase to the surface. When I finally returned to the manor house, my governess said that I looked feverish; my eyes stung with the sweat pouring down from my forehead. But when she asked me what had happened, I said only that I had caught a chill.

I decided to cease any further investigations into whatever my mother and her companions might be doing in their secret underground cavern.

When I grew to be a young man, the gloom and isolation of my mother and her manor house became too oppressive for me to bear. I needed to breathe fresh air, to meet other young men bursting with life. I told her that I wished to travel abroad, to Italy or France, and perhaps also to study at a university. But my mother refused all my entreaties.

In my despair, I turned to the one institution that my mother could not keep me away from without bringing scandal down upon her own head: the Church. Praying every day, I grew friendly with the priest and then, through him, the Bishop and the Abbott of the nearby monastery. I spent more and more of my time with these men of the cloth. While my mother did not hide her scorn for my burgeoning piety, she also did not dare to make enemies of these leaders of the local Church.

One afternoon, I was sitting in the gardens of the monastery with the three clerics. I spoke of how powerfully I felt the presence of Christ and the Holy Spirit in my heart—of how God's love and mercy had brought such joy and light into a soul that had been buried so deeply in sour melancholy. I said that I wished to take my vows to become a novice in the monastery and devote my life to serving God with humility and love.

In response, while they praised my faith, they urged me away from the career of a monk. You are the sole heir to a rich estate and an ancient title, they said, and the Church needs good Christians, men of firm faith, in the nobility—trustworthy men who can guide the Kingdom of Poland in the ways of Christ.

I hung my head and indulged in the kind of petulant outburst that is all too typical of young men with their stormy passions. I swore I could never find happiness in the secular world and especially not in that terrible, gloomy manor house. My only joy in this life was in prayer. Had the Church no pity for a suffering soul like mine?

The three clerics sighed and said that we all must serve Christ with our own unique capacities, even if by doing so we must endure spiritual struggle and hardship. But then the Bishop let something else slip from his tongue. He said: I understand, young man, why you would not wish to return to that house. There are many rumors of your mother's impiety and wickedness. But you must be strong. Someday, you will be lord of that manor. We will help you find a pious Christian wife of the highest birth who will be your helpmeet in cleansing these lands of the foul influence of your mother.

I asked him: What are these rumors? If the fate of my mother's eternal soul hangs in the balance, I must know—perhaps I can persuade her to confess and atone for her sins.

And the Bishop replied: There are rumors that your mother has employed witchcraft to summon the Devil and make an infernal pact with the Evil One. But as there is no firm proof, the Church cannot bring her to trial for her crimes.

Upon hearing these words, I burst into tears, for I had never revealed to my spiritual mentors the horror I had once witnessed in the underground cavern. I suddenly felt that my silence had rendered me complicit in my mother's terrible crimes. Thus, after I had calmed down and steadied myself, I made a full confession of how I had seen my mother leaving that forest path one night and what I had discovered the next day after descending into the cavern. I said that I had been too frightened to speak of these matters before, but now I understood that my soul was at stake and I needed the Church's guidance.

The Bishop said I was wise to be concerned for my soul. But, he added, the testimony I had just given was circumstantial at best. I had not actually seen my mother enter the cavern, much less perform any foul rites there. As there was still no proof that my mother had engaged in acts of sorcery, the Church could not move against a lady of her high rank. Given the seriousness of the matter, he urged me to return to the cavern to secretly observe my mother's conduct there and then report back to him on exactly what she said and did and with what infernal aid and succor.

But he added that he could also appreciate that such a suggestion might be repugnant to the natural affection that a son bears for his mother.

To the contrary, I said, my love for my mother requires that I do whatever is necessary for the salvation of her eternal soul. I promised to do exactly what the Bishop had asked of me and to learn the truth about my mother's ways.

Early that evening, I left our house for one of my solitary walks. With a little bit of effort, I was able to locate again the footpath leading into the woods and to follow it to the artificial grotto carved into the hillside and then down the stairs into the underground cavern. Just as before, the burning stove cast an orange light that allowed me to see clearly across the entire room.

Fortunately, there was still a large pile of crates and barrels lying next to the stove. I hid myself amongst them and waited.

After a time, I heard footsteps on the staircase and then a procession came into view, with my mother in the lead followed by my tutors and governesses. The tutors and governesses lined up against the wall opposite the stove. Then my mother walked towards the cistern filled with water, all the while reciting what seemed to be incantations of some kind in a language I did not understand.

At her approach, the water turned black.

My mother then pronounced another incomprehensible incantation and the darkness faded away to allow a clear picture to emerge on the surface of the water: A man was lying on the floor of a dilapidated hut. He appeared to be an old Jew in a faded caftan with a long, tangled white beard. He was moaning about his sins and begging forgiveness from God. His body was covered in sores and boils and he breathed only with tremendous difficulty. I wanted to turn my eyes away from this hideous sight, but I reminded myself that I was there for the salvation of my mother's soul—I had to muster the strength to do what was needed to save her from the Devil and an eternity of damnation.

My mother then pronounced a new incantation. Suddenly, all the sores and boils on the old Jew's skin burst open and puss and blood streamed forth from his body. He screamed in agony.

And now came the most horrible part: My mother and her companions formed a circle around the cistern, and each one reached into the water with cupped hands, and greedily drank the old Jew's blood and his other secretions. They moaned in ecstasy as their bodies began to glow and hum. Their hair darkened and thickened, and the creases in their skin smoothed out. Their muscles became leaner and firmer.

At some point, my mother and the rest eventually finished what they were doing, stepped back, wiped their chins with their handkerchiefs as if they had just finished devouring a lavish banquet, and processed back out of the cavern in silence.

While I did not understand what I had just witnessed, I knew that this bizarre ritual was something unholy and unchristian. My mother's soul was obviously in the gravest peril and she needed to confess and do penance for her sins as soon as possible—before death carried her away and it would be too late to save her from the flames of perdition.

The next morning, at breakfast, I told my mother that I needed to speak to her about a matter of the utmost importance, but that we must be absolutely alone. Despite the gravity of my tone, she looked at me with a mocking expression in her eyes and seemed on the verge of hurling a sharp insult in my direction. But then she must have changed her mind and she ordered everyone else to leave the room.

Once we were alone, she asked me, in that contemptuous way of hers, to tell her exactly what matter was so pressing and secret.

I then revealed to her all that I had seen during my two trips to her underground cavern. I said that while I did not fully understand these strange rites, they were obviously heretical and demonic. I implored her to think of her eternal soul and to flee from the Devil's embrace to the warm bosom of Our Lord and Savior Jesus Christ. I offered to take her immediately to His Holiness the Bishop so that she could confess her sins and receive instruction on the proper atonement for her crimes.

As soon as I had finished my impassioned plea, she burst out laughing—she cackled like a drunken peasant and nearly fell out of her chair. And as her laughter banged against my ears, I felt humiliated and enraged in equal measure.

I shouted at her to stop—I demanded she stop—which mercifully she did. Then I screamed at her that she was a filthy, lowborn whore and a witch who had sullied my father's pure and ancient noble Christian blood. Her presence in my forefathers' august hall was an insult—worse, an abomination, a sacrilege. I swore that I would cleanse my father's lands of her foul influence.

But then she said, with that grin full of scorn and bile: You understand nothing with your rosary beads and your silly prayers. There is a great God, greater in His power than you can imagine, a fountain of endlessly flowing bounty and wealth and power, but He is so far away that He cannot even see us—we are less than ants to Him, less than worms. Yet there are some special men, including an elect race of saintly Jews, who can, through a genuine, passionate atonement—through a mortification so extreme that it overwhelms all their senses and scatters their reason—become one with the Infinite God in the destruction of their own individual, egoistic, spiritual selves. And once their souls are joined with Him like a drop of water falling into an ocean, His great power concentrates inside them and flows through them, like a funnel. There are very few such men—perhaps only thirty-six in each generation.

That vast power flowing through these saintly Jews can be tapped like a barrel of exquisite wine, should one possess the necessary learning in the occult sciences and a strong enough will.

I have concealed these truths from you because I never intended for you to share in this wondrous bounty. Suffice it to say that I have often theorized that the son of one of these thirty-six Jewish saints could inherit his father's power and be raised and fattened like a spiritual hog for the cunning sorcerer's slaughter.

But I see in your eyes that you do not believe my words—your eyes have the smug, patronizing contempt of a parish priest. Oh, yes, and also that my conduct is an affront to your noble ancestry. Stupid boy, what makes you so sure your blood is exalted? If you wish to know from whose seed you have truly sprung, then you must find a Jew who will tell you a tale of one of their thirty-six hidden saints. When you find the Jew who tells you the right tale, then you will know.

And with that, she laughed again and walked out of the room.

I stormed off and spent the balance of the day walking about in the forest and the fields, seething in my boundless rage. By the time I was sufficiently calm to return to the house, it was already twilight. Still, I was resolved to confront her one last time before revealing what I had learned to the Bishop.

But my mother was gone, along with all my tutors and governesses. The servants said that they had all abruptly departed and did not say where they were going.

I never saw or heard from my mother again. When I went to search for the grotto and the cavern, so as to reveal these demonic marvels to His Holiness the Bishop, they had all vanished, as if the ground had swallowed them up.

And ever since then, when I come across a Jew who is renowned as a storyteller, I ask him for a tale of one of the thirty-six hidden saints.

Now, at last, you, Reb Jacob, have revealed the truth of these dark matters to me.

The nobleman then smiled ruefully and handed a huge fistful of coins to Reb Jacob. Without saying anything more, he left the tavern and walked off alone into the dark night.

Other Books by Barak Bassman

Elegy of the Minotaur

Repentance: A Tale of Demons in Old Jewish Poland

King Solomon and Ashmedai: A Wisdom Tale

The Twilight of the Magical Siren: A Tale of Late Antiquity

The Leper Princess and The Court Jew

The Last Confession of Joseph della Reina

The Gifts of the Fairy Melusine

Necromancy of the Demon Maiden: A Gothic Tale of Podolia

The Death of the Wizard Merlin

The Vampire and The Wandering Jew

The Emissary from Mezeritch: A Dark Hasidic Tale

The Beheading Game: An Arthurian Tale

The Holy Sinner: A Gothic Tale of the Baal Shem Tov

The Abduction of Queen Guinevere

The Cruelty of the Fisher King: A Tale of Perceval and the Holy Grail

The Baal Shem Tov and the Heretic: A Sabbatean Tale

The Starvation Dybbuk: A Cruel Tale of Love and Exorcism

www.ingramcontent.com/pod-product-compliance
Lightning Source LLC
LaVergne TN
LVHW090037080526
838202LV00046B/3852